The Patterdale Terrier

Your Complete Owner's Guide

By Duncan Ross

*All you need to know including
Caring, Grooming, Feeding, Training,
Behaviour and much more!*

Foreword

I remember the very first time I went tagging along with my grandpa on a hunting expedition. We were supposed to be hunting game which included foxes. The thrill of the hunt was indelibly written in my memory, even if we hadn't sighted any fox. But we were usually able to bring home a few hares.

My grandpa owned several foxhounds and two Patterdale Fell Terriers named Ollie and Van. I loved them deeply, and even more so once I had seen them in action during my subsequent hunting trips. So began my love affair with hunting dogs as a whole and of course my favourite, the Patterdale Fell Terrier.

Decades have gone, life took its toll on me. It got me busy with the daily struggles, until now, when I finally sat down and finished this subject very dear to my heart: Patterdale Terriers.

I hope you will love your new pet Patterdale Terrier as much as I have loved my grandpa's dogs and my very own Patterdale from my grandfather's litter.

Acknowledgements

This book is especially dedicated
to the stars in my life:

Ellie Mae

Jacob

Lloyd

Jack

and

Tom

Needless to say,
you inspire me to reach out for the stars
and achieve the goals I have set out to do.

Table of Contents

The Patterdale Terrier

Your Complete Owner's Guide

Your Complete Owner's Guide

Introduction

This book on Patterdale Fell Terriers was written with the utmost consideration for taking the best care of one, understanding the Patterdale Terrier temperament, how to choose one for a pet and so much more.

This book is so comprehensive that you can use it to help you decide if a Patterdale Terrier is indeed well-suited to your lifestyle and needs. Then it will help you pick a Patterdale puppy to adopt or buy. It will even inform you on the pros and cons of adoption, buying from a breeder and buying a pup or an adult dog. You will also learn a lot about how to train and all the specifics of raising your Patterdale Terrier—even the common medical conditions that you should watch out for are included.

Lastly, aside from the important informative sites and associations related to Patterdale Terriers, we have also included a chapter on what to expect from your ageing Patterdale dog and how to take good care of them to make their transition easy.

I know that you will get a lot of informative help from this Patterdale Fell Terrier book and its worth years and years of being, training and working with them.

Chapter 1: What is A Patterdale Terrier?

Terriers are a type of dog breed that are usually small, wiry, fearless and very active. Terriers can range in size from a mere few kilos to as large as over 30 kilos (420 lbs).

The Patterdale Terrier is a breed of dog in the terrier category and it is often also known as the Patterdale Fell Terrier, Patterdale dog, Patterdale dog breed, Patterdale Terrier dog, Patterdale Terrier, Fell Terrier and many other versions of these names.

Terrier History

During the 18th century most terrier breeds were used to control populations of foxes, rabbits and rats, whether under or over the ground. As a matter of fact, bigger sized terriers were used to start badgers from their burrows, and is where the term 'terrier' came from.

The word 'terrier' comes from the Middle French word 'terre' which means 'earth' while the same word in Modern French means 'burrow'.

The 'gameness' of early terriers, especially when it comes to its hunting prowess, were taken advantage of by humans. To choose the best dog breed for its hunting prowess, several types of terrier were tested in a sporting contest where they were placed in an enclosed pit. The fastest dog to kill all the rats within the pit won the contest. The breed's hunting prowess was intensified by selective breeding with specific other breeds to increase the terrier's courage and tenacity.

It is of significant note that the Airedale and Kerry Blue Terrier breeds are especially good in tackling otters in deep water, as well as river rats. On the other hand, Wheaten Terriers were generally tasked as herding dogs. With these capabilities across all terrier breeds, different towns of Great Britain raised and bred terriers that would best suit their needs for vermin control or hunting.

As previously discussed, by the middle of the 19th century and with the coming of dog shows and the sport of dog fighting, terriers were mated with other terrier breeds, fighting dogs and hunting dogs. This refined the terrier breeds from their older, purpose-bred terrier ancestors.

However, it is important and agreeable to note that nowadays, terrier breeds are primarily bred as pets and companion dogs. Generally terriers are affectionate and loyal to their owners, but they may have a 'devious' streak in them which would need a firm hand.

Types of Terriers

Currently there are several special groups of terriers, each group comprising several breeds. Some of the terrier groupings are not scientific but classified by kennel clubs, or sometimes categorised by their function or size to make it simple for breeders, pet-owners and would-be pet-owners alike. In 18th century Britain, terriers were segregated into two types: short-legged and long-legged.

If we were to classify terriers according to function and size, this is how it would go:

- **Bull Type Terriers** – from the name itself, most dog lovers would recognise that this is a kind of breed combination between a terrier and a bulldog. It's sad to admit that this type of terrier breed (which encompasses the Asian Gull Terrier, Staffordshire Bull Terrier, American Pit Bull

Terrier and Bull Terrier, among others) are still bred for the illegal dog fighting industry.

- **Toy Terriers** – Example breeds of this type of terrier are the Yorkshire Terrier and the English Toy Terrier. Although these dogs are small, they have maintained much of their original terrier character and are not just submissive lap dogs. The companion or toy group terriers are a smaller rendition of their larger terrier ancestors.

- **Working Terriers** – These are the hunting breed of terriers and this is where the Patterdale Terrier belongs, along with the West Highland Terrier, Scottish Terrier, Cairn Terrier, Jack Russell Terrier and others. This terrier dog breed is used for finding, tracking, trailing and bolting quarry— even quarries that live underground. The working terriers are further divided into two, which are the hunt terriers and the fell terriers. The former are terrier breeds created to bolt, kill or locate foxes in a traditional fox hunt; these breeds originated in Southern England. The latter—fell terriers—were bred in Northern England to help in killing foxes and this is where Patterdale Terriers specifically belong.

Patterdale Terrier History

Patterdale Terrier history goes way back to the first part of the 20th century. It is considered to be an English dog breed originating from the Northern Terrier breeds. Specifically, it was an early border hunt master, Joe Bowman, who originated the breed. He was a hunt master living in Ullswater in the Lake District of Northern England.

Patterdale Terrier history started with the idea of breeding a terrier to hunt and dispatch red fox in the rocky fells of the area—which means that the typical digging terrier was not hugely useful in this case.

The place where Patterdale Terriers were line bred by Joe Bowman is too hilly and unsuitable for arable farming, so the primary form of livelihood in the area is sheep farming and the rearing small animals. In this kind of industry, farmers believe that foxes are the primary predator that they are up against, and this is where Patterdale Terrier dogs are so valuable. Patterdale Terriers are the indisputable leader in performance and number when it comes to fell terrier breeds. So Patterdale Terriers were bred for predator control of the farmer's livestock, such as sheep.

The rocky dens and terrain of the Lake District of Northern England was very different from the dirt dens of the hunting terrain in the South. This difference in terrain meant that the terrier had to be capable of dispatching the fox wherever it was found or the ability to bolt the fox from a rocky crevice.

Patterdale Terrier Characteristics

You might wonder how big a Patterdale Terrier is. The Patterdale Terrier is generally between 10 and 15 inches (25 – 38cm) in height. The Patterdale Terrier's weight ranges from 15 to 30 pounds (7 to 14 kilos). Plus it should be in fit and working condition.

Patterdale Terrier Statistics:

Height: 10 – 15" (25 – 38cm)
Weight: 15 – 30 lbs (7 – 14 kg)

The United Kennel Club in the United States, which is the kennel club that accepts Patterdale Terrier breeds as legitimate, has placed a standard on the breed. The Patterdale dog must have a balanced and compact appearance. For the Patterdale dog to be a working terrier, it must be able to follow quarry and be able to squeeze through very small and perhaps even underground passages. Aside from this capability, a Patterdale dog should also have a strong neck and the stamina to hold its quarry at bay. All in all, a Patterdale dog should have great endurance and flexibility.

Your Complete Owner's Guide

Overall Description

Among the Patterdale Terrier characteristics are that it is a powerful and strong dog—which is perfectly balanced with the Patterdale Terrier size. When viewed from the front the Patterdale will look like a trapezoid or shaped like a wedge.

The size of the muzzle of a Patterdale Terrier is a bit smaller than the skull. Its muzzle and jowl will be fairly well built.. The Patterdale dog breeds' muzzle is not weak or snippy; instead it should be strong along with strong white teeth that come with a level or scissor bite. As a prospective Patterdale owner, you need to know that broken incisors or teeth that are lost due to working should not be punished.

Eyes – the eyes of the Patterdale dog breed must be in agreement with the coat colour of the terrier—but they are never coloured blue. The eyes should also be fairly wide apart and squarely set in the skull. Since the Patterdale dog breed is an earth-working dog, it is crucial that its eyes should not bulge or protrude.

Ears – the tips of the ears should sit directly outside the corner of the eye. They should be moderate to small in size and triangular in shape. The Patterdale dog breed's ears should lightly fold just above its skull.

Nose – most Patterdale dog breeds' noses are black, except for the chocolate, brown or liver coloured Patterdale, which all have a red nose.

Neck & Shoulders – The neck of the Patterdale dog breed is of moderate length and muscular. It slowly widens from the nape to smoothly blend with the terrier's shoulders.

Forelegs & Hind Legs – The forelegs of Patterdale Terriers have good bone structure and are straight and strong. The elbows are located close to the body but can still freely move. The pasterns are flexible and powerful. The hindquarters are both muscular and strong. Their musculature, angulation and bone should equal the forelegs. The hocks are well let down and the stifles well bent. When the Patterdale Terrier is standing, the strong and short rear pasterns should be perpendicular to the floor; and if this is viewed from the back they would look parallel to each other.

Body – the Patterdale Terrier's body is square-shaped and marginally longer than its height. The body is measured from the shoulder point to the buttocks point along with the point from the withers to the ground.

Back – the back of a Patterdale Terrier should be of moderate level and length. It should blend into a slightly arched and muscular loin which has a moderate to slight tuck up.

Chest & Spanning – The chest should be deep, nearly up to the level of the elbow. It is flexible yet firm. It must be oval in shape and moderate in width. An important proportion for judging Patterdale Terriers is spanning. The Patterdale dog must be spanned which will test its flexibility, compression and size. The Patterdale Terrier must be spanned by an average man's hands directly behind the shoulders. When spanning a Patterdale dog, you have to lift the front legs off the ground as you gently squeeze the bottom of the chest to ensure that the chest will compress.

Tail – the tail is never carried over the back, but instead is set high. If the tail is to be docked, only one half to one third of the tail must be removed. This is because there will be times that the only way of pulling your terrier out of a burrow is by tugging at his tail. The tail should not be overly thick but must be strong. There is no preferred tail; both natural and docked are suitable for Patterdale Terriers.

Patterdale Breed Coat

The Patterdale dog breed can have three different types of coat: rough, broken or smooth. However, all these types of coat should have coarse and dense double coats which feel harsh to the touch and are quite weatherproof.

Let's get into details about the Patterdale dog breed coats:

- **Rough** – the Patterdale dog with a rough coat will have overall longer hair on its muzzle, ears and face. It will also have guard or trace hair on its body, legs, face and head. It will also have a very protective and thick double coat. The Patterdale dog's rough coat is not woolly or soft. Instead it is harsh, to provide itself with ample protection from the elements. The great thing about Patterdale dogs with rough coats is that they do not shed which makes them a great pet candidate for those who have allergies. The rough coat would need sporadic plucking or stripping. A properly groomed rough Patterdale dog coat will be bristly.

- **Broken** – the Patterdale dog with a broken coat will show an outward coarse coat with a bit of lengthier coat upon its body while its ears and head coat is smooth. The broken coat is quite like a smooth coat but will have coarser and longer hair on the body. The ears and the face will have a smooth coat with a trace of guard hair on the feet, chin and muzzle. The Patterdale Terrier's broken coat will be largely dense, hard and flat. Generally, a broken coat will need a quick tidying up and minimal grooming. Finally, the broken coat is harsh rather than soft so that it can give

the Patterdale
Terrier sufficient
protection from
the elements.

- **Smooth** – the
  Patterdale dog
  with a smooth coat
  will have glossy,
  short hair. The
  undercoat is
  almost always
  present. It should
  not be soft or
  sparse and should
  provide the
  Patterdale dog ample protection from the
  elements. Further, a smooth coated Patterdale
  dog will not have any guard or trace hair on its
  body, legs, face, nose or head. In addition, the
  coat should be uniform and short in length.
  Lastly, the smooth coat will not require any
  grooming at all.

Patterdale Dog Breed Colour

The Patterdale dog breed comes in several different colours, such as:

- **Black Patterdale Terrier** – a black Patterdale dog will have dark black fur. However,  there are also variations of black available, such as with gold, red or brown highlights.

- **Brown Patterdale Terrier, Chocolate Patterdale Terrier or Liver Coloured Patterdale** – brown or chocolate coloured Patterdale dogs will have an officially "red" nose which is sometimes referred to as a liver-coloured nose.

- **Red Patterdale Terrier** – most red Patterdale dogs will have a black nose.

- **Black and Tan Patterdale Terrier** – this is any variation of a tan coloured Patterdale dog with black markings like a black saddle on its back or a black mask on the muzzle.

There are cases when Patterdale dogs can come in brindle colours but never fully in white. Some white patches on the feet or chest of the Patterdale Terrier is acceptable, but if white patches occur away from the mentioned sites, this would mean that the dog has been crossbred. This happens particularly with the Patterdale Terrier and Jack Russell Terrier mix.

Patterdale Terrier Personality

The Patterdale Terrier personality is laid back and not as yappy as other terrier breeds. It tends to enjoy warm places like curling up at the heating duct inside the home.

Even though the Patterdale Terrier's size is sufficient for it to be qualified as a toy dog, its gameness and ability makes it a solid terrier. The Patterdale dog's toughness and determination excludes him from the mastiff group of dogs.

Patterdale Terriers are tough and game during hunting periods and this is the main

reason why hunters take three to four dogs during hunting.

The Patterdale is also a good guard dog but is not a good pet for the faint of heart or for the non-terrier fan. Therefore, it is not recommended for the average pet owner. Patterdale dogs would need mind challenges, including a lot of physical exercise. Patterdale dogs have a keen sense and can easily figure out if you are strong minded or not. If you are deemed as not strong-minded, the Patterdale Terrier will think that it is alpha and will give its owners a handful.

Patterdale Terriers are independent and robust hunters who were bred solely for functional services as a hunting champion and a ratter. Due to its bull terrier pedigree, this makes the Patterdale dog way too fierce to function as a hunter along with pack hounds.

Moreover, Patterdale Terriers are especially persistent and hard. So you might want to be careful around foxhound owners because your pet terrier will probably bolt their fox, or worse, kill it! This is also the top reason why Patterdales are unlikely bed fellows with pack hounds because its instincts will tell it to kill a fox rather than let it bolt, which therefore spoils the hunt for the hounds.

Another great Patterdale Terrier personality is its excellent digging skills. It will be intent on tracking and digging to attack and kill any mammal that has burrowed into the ground to hide. The fells of Northern

Britain have filled (and still do fill) the need for them to hunt foxes. In this territory, scree, mines, and rock tips afford foxes protection and only a Patterdale Terrier is fearless enough to go to ground and effective enough to scramble over this terrain.

As a prospective Patterdale pet owner, you also need to know that with the Patterdale Terrier personality, which is not obedient to training, will be a handful to raise. You should also know that Patterdale Terriers should not be left to mingle with other non-canine pets.

Take good care of your small Patterdale dog because due to their confidence and boldness, they are known to chase animals that are far bigger than themselves. Many a Patterdale pup has been killed when chasing raccoons into their dens when out on a casual walking exercise with their owner.

In order to avoid behavioural problems from your Patterdale pet, you have to be a consistent, confident and firm pack leader and provide them with plenty of mental activities. Lastly, do not permit your Patterdale Terrier to acquire the Small Dog Syndrome (you can get more information on this in Chapter 9).

Living Conditions

With the Patterdale Terrier personality and traits, it is not advisable to get this kind of pet when you live in an apartment—Patterdales are not well-suited to life in an apartment.

Patterdale dogs are quite well-behaved indoors, provided that they get enough exercise during the day. The Patterdale breed can also be housed along with two to three other dogs, provided that it gets enough hunting and exercise to keep it content; if not, the Patterdale dog can get bored and will easily pick a fight with the dogs housed alongside it.

Do They Make Good Pets?

This is the million dollar question that you are waiting to be answered. All in all, if you are a newbie pet owner, then my advice to you is to look for other dog breeds that are easily trained and managed. If you do not have experience with pets, you might easily get disheartened with the Patterdale Terrier personality, not because it is unlovable, but because you lack the necessary experience, understanding and patience.

If you are looking for a companion pet, the Patterdale Terrier may or may not be a good choice for you. However, if you are a hunter and are looking for a hunting companion, then getting a Patterdale Terrier as a pet and hunting companion is ideal for you.

In essence, when answering a question of this magnitude, it all boils down to what you need. What are you looking for in a pet? This is the main reason why I have placed all the general information on Patterdale Terriers in chapter one so that you can get to know this dog breed.

Is the size and weight of this dog what you are looking for? If yes, then that's a good point and get on to the next questions. Do you live in an apartment? If you do, then I don't recommend getting a Patterdale dog.

Are you looking for an energetic exercise companion? If yes, then this is the dog that you are looking for. The final question of great importance is: are you capable of being the "top dog" and bringing this Patterdale Terrier to heel?" If you answer no to this question, then my advice to you is to please save yourself from the stress and anxiety. But if you do have a lot of time and effort on your hands and are up to this challenge, then go for it.

On the other hand, if you have the right behaviour and can provide ample stimulation and exercise to your pet Patterdale Terrier, you will find that it is quite a suitable pet for a large family or a sole owner.

How Much Do They Cost?

The current selling rate of Patterdale Terrier dogs is between $250 and $500 (£150 and £300). Usually you would have to send a 50% deposit and will need to pick up your pup from the owner's place. However, there are also ways to have your pup shipped to you, but this has highly been discouraged because it is best if you get to inspect your would-be pet firsthand. You will learn more about buying Patterdale Terriers in the next chapter.

The Patterdale Terrier and Cats

This is an age old question that we instinctively know the answer to, but still hope for a ceasefire. In all honesty, dogs and cats do not mix and the more energetic and the smaller the dog, the higher is the dog's dislike for cats. So as a general rule of thumb, Patterdale Terriers and cats do not mix.

However, you might have heard and read conflicting and varying advice about Patterdale Terriers and cats. This would be the usual scenario if you mix your Patterdale Terrier and cat: more often than not, your Patterdale dog will give instant chase to the cat once the pooch sees it. The cat will be chased around the house until it stops—when the pooch cannot reach the cat; 99% of the time, your Patterdale Terrier and cat will walk away from this incident until the next one occurs.

If you really want to mix a Patterdale Terrier and a cat, do not be disheartened as there are ways and occurrences where dogs and cats have been documented to live alongside each other harmoniously. You will learn some tips and tricks on how to do this later in the book.

Chapter 2. Understanding the Patterdale Terrier as a Pet

It is important to know and understand that Patterdale puppies are not a perfect fit for everyone. Therefore you need to understand well the Patterdale Terrier temperament in order to get along with it well and it can become your new family companion.

You need to understand that a Patterdale pup is highly driven, fearless and smart, therefore it needs to be trained thoroughly. Training of your Patterdale pooch will be discussed in detail in succeeding chapters.

Understanding Your Patterdale Pup's Temperament and Activities

Despite all these warnings, a Patterdale Terrier pup is an extremely loving pet. With the right time, care, training and conditions, it will bond strongly to its owner and the family as a whole. For most Patterdale owners, the true value of the Patterdale pets lie in their temperament. The Patterdale pup temperament combines the best characteristics of a working, hunting and companion dog without compromise. Here is a quick list of the Patterdale dog's rewarding temperament and abilities:

- naturally becomes a part of the family
- affectionate
- loyal
- easy to train
- eager to please
- intelligent
- elite hunting breed
- ability to tunnel
- capable of hunting game that has gone to ground
- ability to hunt rats, rabbits, foxes, marmots, raccoons, and wild boar, among others
- it can kill or bolt game
- an excellent guard dog
- its coat is perfect for those who have sensitive noses and have allergies to dog fur

Patterdales as Companion Dogs

The Patterdale temperament found in the UK seems to be primarily focused on hunting and eradicating nuisance farmer pests; in the USA, Patterdale puppies are more and more kept as a companion dog; this is because Patterdale Terrier pups will stay with you as you go around the house doing chores and can remain quiet.

Your Complete Owner's Guide

There are many reports of households who have successfully incorporated a Patterdale dog into their family. These families have reported that indeed they love having a Patterdale as pet and vice versa. These Patterdale dogs are alright living with children; however, for really young kids, supervision is necessary, just like with any other dog breed. Patterdale pups will leave the vicinity of an overly enthusiastic child, given the choice; but if it is cornered a Patterdale dog can bite.

Aside from kids, Patterdale pups have been shown to live harmoniously with cats—this is especially true if the Patterdale Terrier and cat have lived together since the Patterdale was a pup. This kind of relationship between Patterdale Terrier and cat must be enforced by the owner and the owner must train both Patterdale Terrier and cat to live peaceably together.

Patterdales as Hunting Dogs

Now, if you're looking for a Patterdale that you want to help you with your hunting expeditions, then you have made a wise choice.

Since Patterdales can socialise with any type of dog

breed, you can definitely add this pet to your growing list of pets. If you already have a Patterdale dog, then it is not a problem to add another Patterdale dog to your litter, or another dog breed for that matter. However, you may encounter problems with mixing in other furry and scurrying creatures into your list of pets because your Patterdale pups' hunting instinct is sure to be on alert.

Your Patterdale pup will indeed love chasing small animals (whether you are out hunting or just walking) like large birds, pigeons and squirrels. Once your pet Patterdale gets its prey, it will definitely kill the creature. Another thing that you should know is that your pet terrier will definitely chase, in a ferocious fashion, a fox if it ever sees one. Often, your pet Patterdale may not reach the fox in time, but I advise you not to encourage such behaviour because this may lead to the death of your precious pet.

It has been reported that in fights between a fox and a Patterdale Terrier, the odds of winning are 50-50 which is therefore an uncertain predicament for your precious pet. What other hunting owners do is own two Patterdale dogs (especially if they are keen on fox hunting) so that the outcome of the battle tips unanimously in the Patterdale Terrier's favour.

You may begin to wonder and question, can I not have both a hunting and companion Patterdale Terrier pet? Yes, of course you can. However, you would need to understand that the Patterdale Terrier temperament may be feisty and that you will have a limited choice of having other pets within the home.

Having a well-behaved Patterdale Terrier, both as a hunting dog and a companion pet, boils down to your training skills, time and effort put into raising your pet Patterdale Terrier the way you hope it would grow—and the only way to do this is to arm yourself with knowledge.

Tips to Follow & Common Mistakes to Avoid

Here is an in-depth rundown of the common mistakes you must avoid when choosing a pet Patterdale, when getting ready for owning your Patterdale pup and so much more. Basically these quick tips will be useful to you as a present or future owner of a Patterdale Terrier puppy.

- You are forewarned not to leave your young Patterdale Terrier puppy alone for lengthy periods of time because this pooch does not fit the conventional meaning of a couch potato, lap dog or even a yard art—something will go amiss in the end.

- Indubitably, Patterdale Terrier puppies are a very handsome breed and its appearance gives the effect of getting a big dog's temperament, neatly presented in a small package; but you have to remember this, the Patterdale Terrier puppies are not mini-labs. Therefore, choosing Patterdales as pets solely based on its appearance is not a very good idea.

- Before you buy a Patterdale puppy and bring it to the house, you first should already have a well-rounded strategy for the Patterdale puppies' protection, caring and training. Plus, you or a member of the family should arm yourself with knowledge on Patterdale Terriers.

- Before buying a Patterdale Terrier puppy, you need to painstakingly understand the breed. Furthermore, it would also be a great idea to buy your pup from a knowledgeable breeder who can lend you support and guidance in raising your pet Patterdale Terrier breed—which definitely requires training skills and time.

- Once you have decided that you are ready to own and raise a Patterdale Terrier pup as pet, this is when your relationship with your pet begins. From the moment that you bring your new Patterdale pet into your home, you are responsible for it—for all its needs. Your choice of training, goals, expectations, housing and feeding will eventually govern the quality of your relationship with your pet Patterdale.

- Remember that the all too important key to raising the best in the Patterdale dog temperament is its early socialization with livestock, dogs and people.

- Since Patterdale Terriers have inherent hunting instincts, they should not be mixed with other pets that are their natural prey or somehow looks and acts like their prey. If that other pet is furry, runs, scurries, hides or burrows—then it's definitely an instinctive prey for Patterdale Terriers; this is especially true for Patterdale pets that have not been trained in socialising.

- This has already been mentioned in the first chapter, but again I repeat: apartment living is not suitable for Patterdale Terriers because of their inherent thirst and love for physical exercise and activity plus engaging brain activities too. The lack of physical and intellectual exercise and activity for the Patterdale pup is usually the culprit behind bad behaviour.

- Patterdale Terriers are responsive to training, but they are NOT lap dogs. So, anticipate a bit of frustration when training your Patterdale pet because they have a lot of sneaky tricks up their sleeves. As one owner have commented: *"They will also often frustrate even highly skilled & experienced professionals, since they can go off unexpectedly like aging nitroglycerin, or sometimes appear to forget they ever learned the exercise at all, or find a brand-new twist on their 'compliance' that they haven't tried yet. And they try it out in the ring, with the stands packed, to the crowd's delight and the handler's horror."* And this is what makes Patterdale Terriers endearing to their owners. *"They'll keep you guessing, wondering, laughing and often swearing—but they won't bore you."*

- Another important tip: remember that Patterdale Terriers do not only need Physical exercise—they also need mental stimulation. After physical exercise Patterdale Terriers will be mentally alert and at a high stage of excitement—so you also have to provide your pet with mental stimulus in order to tire it and keep it quiet.

- Did you know that terriers have no road sense? Yes, Patterdale Terriers are oblivious to the dangers of traffic and may run the risk of getting hit by a car all because of its hunting senses on overdrive when chasing a squirrel or whatnot. Remember this vulnerability of a Patterdale Terrier and protect it from undue risks.

- Protect your Patterdale Terrier pup from getting lost by micro chipping them (you will learn more about this advance technology in a later chapter). Also, let your dog wear its Dog ID tag at all times. You would never know when, where, how or why your Patterdale Terrier puppy would bolt away from you.

Patterdale-Proof Your Home

In order to create a safe environment for your Patterdale pups, you have to Patterdale-proof your home. Not only are you protecting your pet Patterdale Terrier pups, you are also protecting yourself from any untoward damage to your property.

Let me tell you stories of Patterdale dog owners who did not dog-proof their home. I hope with these stories, you will learn valuable lessons from their experiences.

A friend of a friend told me this story a few years back regarding another friend who lost his Patterdale Terrier puppy in a very sad way. The Patterdale Terrier pup was able to take hold of a bottle of Advil, chewed off the cap and continued to eat the rest of the tablets inside. Needless to say, the dog died. This kind of accident could have easily been avoided if the home was dog-proofed.

In another story that I read on the internet, although the dog was not a Patterdale Terrier puppy but another dog breed, it cost a lot of money on medical bills for their pet dog. The Dachshund chewed plugged electrical cords in the home and led to flesh and skin burns in the mouth of the dog. If only those electrical cords had been kept out of reach or the home had simply been dog-proofed, the Dachshund's owner wouldn't have to pay the vet's bill of $10,000 (£6,000).

These are real stories from real dog owners who did not dog-proof their homes, which shows us why this is an important stage that you need to fulfill before your Patterdale Terrier puppies arrive.

Dog-Proof the House as You Would If You Had a Baby

Patterdale Terrier puppies are just like human babies, very inquisitive and with no idea of the danger they are in. So whatever keeps a child safe in the home will also keep your pet Patterdale pooch safe—this is a general rule of thumb.

Here's a quick run down of the important items that you may need to install to keep your Patterdale Terrier puppy safe.

- A safe place to contain your electrical cords and wires. It should be kept in a place where your dog cannot reach it; if this is not possible then you may need to invest in a container that is sturdy enough to withstand a Patterdale's gnawing.

- Safety locks for all your cabinets in the kitchen, bedrooms, bathrooms, and wherever there are cabinets in the home—especially those that are within reach of your Patterdale Terrier puppy.

- Covers for your extension leads and electrical outlets. You would never know what goes on in the head of your Patterdale puppy. It's better to be safe than sorry.

- Installation of baby gates will also be helpful in keeping your dog from entering rooms where he is not allowed.

- Put away hazardous chemicals, cleaning products and any type of medication. Keep it tightly sealed and closed—away from the reaches of your terrier.

Clean Your Clutter

Let's face it, Patterdale Terrier puppies, or any dog breed for that matter, love to chew on things. If your home is filled with clutter, just imagine that clutter multiplying itself a thousandfold... Not a very nice scenario right? Not only that, you would be crying buckets of tears if your beloved shades, your favorite designer shoes or other personal effects were suddenly ripped to pieces—nothing will be safe from your Patterdale's jaws.

So, get smart, tidy up and if you have been planning to organise your home for a while, now would be the right time.

Invest in a Dog-Proof Rubbish Bin

You have no idea how Patterdale Terrier puppies can get into trouble with rubbish. For these dogs, the litter bin is a treasure trove of yummy goodies like fast food wrappers, used tissues, pizza crusts and many other delicious treats.

Not only can this rubbish be a source of cleaning headache for you, it can also be the ultimate money guzzling pit! You ask why? Well, your litter bin could be a source of intestinal blockage for your pet which is a costly medical problem. Your pet could even have diarrhoea from all those nasty food smelling items that you have in the rubbish and Patterdale diarrhoea is not a nice sight to see and to clean!

My suggestion would be a pullout rubbish bin which would need two things: an under the counter space and money, because a pullout rubbish bin means ££££. Since Patterdale Terrier dogs are relatively small, you can also invest in a step-on lid metal rubbish bin.

Invest in a Dog Food Vault

A dog food vault is a safe container that your Patterdale Terrier puppy cannot open or reach. Having one in the house is definitely a must since Patterdale puppies are quite crafty.

However, having a dog-proof dog food container is not enough! You have to remember to put the lid tightly on, or else it's quite easy for your pooch to work the lid off.

Close All Entry/Exit Points

There are basically two reasons why you would want to manage the entry and exit points. The first reason is to keep your Patterdale Terrier puppy from getting lost in the jungle city that you call home. The second reason is to keep your Patterdale Terrier puppies from gaining entry into bedrooms and causing havoc to your personal belongings.

The first point of entry or exit is inside the home whether through the door, garage or gate. These entry points keep your Patterdale Terrier puppies inside your garden or the immediate vicinity of your home where you know that they will not get lost.

There are so many reported cases of lost Patterdale Terriers who have bolted out of the home or car. The worst case scenario that you can think of is your pet bolting across the street and getting run over by a car.

So, some key access point into and out of the house that you must monitor and manage are: car doors, garden, back gate, house windows, front door, back door, garage door and any access that is within 200 yards of a road.

The next point of entry that you need to check is the doors within the home. This time, you are protecting your property from your mischievous Patterdale Terrier puppy. You wouldn't want to be surprised as you collapse on a wet bed as it is not a comforting predicament, nor is seeing your bedroom linen in a shambles.

So learn to close all the doors to rooms at all times. And the rule of thumb in your home should be: keep your dog in a place where it can do no harm to itself or to your stuff—this is where baby gates are very helpful. Lastly, if you aren't in a room that has a door, your Patterdale puppy shouldn't be in there either.

Identify and Store Patterdale Hazardous Items

You need to know and understand that the biological makeup of Patterdale Terrier puppies or any dog breed for that matter is different from humans. What may be considered as food for humans can be a toxic killer for dogs. So, here is a list of common items found in our home that are actually toxic to our pooches:

- chocolate
- alcoholic drinks
- coffee grounds
- cigarettes
- potpourri oils
- medications
- fabric softener sheets
- mothballs
- mouse and rat poisons
- antifreeze
- pesticides
- house plants such as hyacinth, philodendron and dieffenbachia to name but a few.

Most of the objects mentioned above are easily part of any home, so please be careful with these things when you have a pet Patterdale around and be sure to store these away from your pet dog's reach. As for the plants, I recommend that you throw these away and try to look for other plant species to cultivate to protect you Patterdale puppy from medical harm.

Chapter 3. Buying Your Pet Patterdale Terrier Dog

Nowadays there are so many furores about buying Patterdale Fell terriers—well most dog breeds for that matter—because a lot of animal rights activists are pushing for dog adoption rather than buying a Patterdale pup.

Adopting a Patterdale Fell terrier is also called rehoming or fostering. As an insider in the dog rescue world, it is quite astounding to know that hundreds of thousands of dogs are looking to find a new home. And the most heart wrenching fact is that, some of them are going to be put to sleep—forever—a few days from now.

Adopting a Patterdale Fell Terrier

Adoption should be one of your first choices when looking for a pet Patterdale Fell Terrier—or for any dog breed for that matter. Pet rescue and shelters are over flowing with rescued dogs because previous owners had to move, got divorced or simply ran out of money or time to care for their pet. So, here are a handful of benefits why adopting a Patterdale Terrier would be advantageous for you.

Advantages of Adoption

- Adopting a Patterdale Fell Terrier would certainly be cheaper than buying a Patterdale pup.

- With Patterdale Terrier adoption you can have your dream pet right away; unlike with buying a Patterdale Terrier puppy, often you have to wait for months to get your pup. There will also be cases where you will have to reserve your pup, even before it has been born.

- With adoption, you can choose Patterdale Fell Terrier puppies that have already been house trained by its previous owner. This means that it's less work for you in terms of training.

- Patterdale Fell Terriers, especially coming from a shelter, would have already been tested for heartworm and provided with preventative medication.

- Your adopted Patterdale Terrier puppy will be treated for mites, ticks and fleas.

- Your adopted Patterdale Terrier puppy will also be vaccinated for rabies

- Your Patterdale Terrier puppy will also have received a veterinary examination and health screening, which will give you a guarantee that your adopted pet will not die within a few days of rehoming.

- There are also shelters that provide follow-up support after adopting your Patterdale pet. This support can be: pet sitting, referrals to experienced good grooming services, dog training classes and counselling for certain behaviours.

- And most of all, you are saving a life!

Disadvantages of Adoption

- The history of the desired Patterdale Terrier in the shelter is often times unknown. However, there are previous owners who provide the dog with its history like: vaccination records, health history, temperament and lineage.

- Some dogs in the shelter may have been neglected or abused and stressed Patterdale Terrier traits will be affected and they may act differently in normal circumstances.

- There will be shelters that have lengthy application times because they want to ensure that the potential Patterdale Terrier owner has understood the time and effort it entails in bringing up a pet. The shelter also wants to ensure that interaction between the potential owner and dog is getting stronger. The shelter will also want to protect these sheltered animals from further abuse or neglect or disappointment from being returned to the shelter again and again.

Tips and Tricks in Adopting a Patterdale Fell Terrier

- Facilities may have different policies with regards to interacting with the potential Patterdale pet terrier. But the idea is that you and your family or other household pets should interact with the possible Patterdale dog before adopting it so that you will have an optimal match.

- If you have already found a suitable Patterdale Terrier dog to adopt, ask all the necessary questions that you would want to know. Putting off the adoption at a later time can result in the dog being no longer available by then; because animal rescue groups can temporarily house animals at another location for medical care, additional training or other reasons.

- Remember that when adopting a Patterdale Fell Terrier its full history is often unavailable, plus the fact that you may have a limited time to decide whether to adopt or not.

Buying a Patterdale Fell Terrier

When buying a Patterdale pet, usually people would consider getting their first puppy from the pet shop or from a breeder. However, before I teach you how to shop for the perfect Patterdale Terrier puppy, as much as possible, let me give you the different pros and cons of buying from a pet shop and from a breeder.

Pros and Cons of Buying from a Pet Shop

A lot of people dissuade potential pet owners from buying a pet dog—any breed—from a pet shop for humane reasons. But, studies have further proven that pet shops are not a good source for your Patterdale pet terrier because of the following issues:

- excitability
- harder to train
- touch sensitivity problems
- fearful
- soiling issues

Furthermore, Patterdale Fell Terriers are a rare breed of dog, so more often than not, pet shops do not carry this breed. So your only chance of buying a Patterdale Terrier puppy is from a reputable breeder.

Choosing the Right Patterdale Terrier Breeder

- Just like with any dog breeder, your chosen Patterdale Terrier breeders should be well-respected and responsible. You will be confident that a Patterdale Terrier breeder is responsible because they will always be concerned about the betterment of the breed and not just cranking out more money.

- It is also advisable that you go and check out Patterdale breeders and visit them in their home or establishment to check out the quality of the environment. If you notice that the pets are in cages, it's best to steer clear of these Patterdale Terrier breeders because Patterdale dogs—or any breed of dog for that matter—that are brought up in cages are no different from the ones in a pet shop. They will have Patterdale Terrier trait issues. This is commonly because a cage-reared Patterdale pup won't be exposed to new situations or doesn't get enough handling. It excretes, sleeps, and eats in a small area which totally goes against its instincts; resulting in a poorly socialised, fearful or shy Patterdale dog.

- Communicate with your Patterdale Terrier breeder. The communication should flow freely and you shouldn't feel that you are being interrogated or awkward. You also need to understand that a good breeder will ask questions about you because they are like loving parents to their Patterdale pups who also want to ensure that they are going to a good home.

- A good Patterdale breeder will also be knowledgeable on Patterdale Terrier traits and will not mind sharing information or his or her knowledge about them, which will ensure a smooth and happy transition of the Patterdale puppy into its new owner's home.

- Often Patterdale Terrier breeders will put future pups on sale and will wait list potential buyers. So throughout the waiting time, from the time you have voiced out your decision to buy a Patterdale pup until such time as the pup is ready to be weaned away from its mother, your Patterdale Terrier breeder should keep you involved in the process.

How to Choose a Healthy Patterdale Puppy

Before choosing your pet from a Patterdale Terrier breeder, ensure that you have seen it first-hand. Buying long-distance and just having the pup shipped to your location is a big no-no because chances are you haven't seen the health of these Patterdale puppies and you might be given a sickly—or worse—a dying one!

So here are some key Patterdale dog features that you should check:

- Check the Patterdale Terrier puppy for chronic sneezing or coughing.

- Check the Patterdale Terrier puppy for discharges from its rear end.

- Check the Patterdale Terrier puppy's belly. Generally, all puppies will be a bit potbellied especially when full; however, a puppy with an obviously swollen tummy is a positive indication of a worm infestation.

- The Patterdale Terrier puppy's coat should be shiny and clean.

- The Patterdale Terrier puppy's nose and eyes should not be runny or red but clean and clear.

- As for the Patterdale Terrier traits, this is really common sense. If you find a cowering and timid pup, it will grow up to be shy. If you choose a friendly and bright puppy, it will continue to be a friendly and bright dog.

- Another key in finding the right Patterdale Terrier dog for you is to ensure that the puppy should also be interested in you and not just you in him. You can easily test this by doing the belly-up posture, which is a form of submission in dogs, and cradle the pup like a baby. If the pup fights you, then that pup is one of the dominant pups of the litter or it could also be one of the less trustful ones. Do the same for the other pups in the litter. Also, try it a few times at different stages of interaction because just like humans, Patterdale pups can also experience mood swings.

- Ensure you have a look at both parents of the puppy you are considering buying. They should give a good indication of how your dog will turn out once it reaches adulthood.

WARNING: You may have a soft heart and would just go right ahead and buy a sickly puppy which you believe would get better with time and care. However, I want to warn you that a sickly Patterdale puppy will have major health problems once it's all grown up. This means that your veterinary bills can easily go sky high; so, if you are not well-equipped—financially, emotionally and even time wise—please don't bother with sickly dogs.

Chapter 4: Care Instructions for your Pet Patterdale Terrier

Patterdale Terriers are the most robust of all types of working terriers. They have solid legs and are predisposed to have better health than other dogs.

Moreover, they are less fussy compared to other types of terriers. Although Patterdale Terriers do not require high maintenance like other dogs, it is still important that you know how to properly take care of them so that they will be able to live a happy and meaningful doggy life.

There are certain things that you need to take note of when you decide to have Patterdale Terriers as pets and these include their physical needs for space, food, grooming, wellness and training. In this chapter you will be taught everything that you need to know about care of the Patterdale Terrier breed. Each section will give you an in-depth discussion on how you will be able to successfully care for your Patterdale Terrier dog.

Grooming

The best thing about this type of breed is that they have short, rough coats of fur and therefore require little grooming (unlike long-haired toy dogs); thus grooming for the Patterdale breed can be very easy. Moreover, Patterdale Terrier shedding is not very common, unlike many other types of dog. Here are the things that you need to be aware of when it comes to grooming your Patterdale Terrier working dogs.

A. Hair

One of the most convenient of all Patterdale Terrier traits is its short hair, thus you do not need to have your dog trimmed during the summer months or fear that the hair will grow too long. To groom the hair, all you need is a curry comb and a chamois cloth to remove the loose hair from your dog. When brushing your dog's fur, it is important that you do not pull hard to prevent hurting your dog. Although it is rare for its fur to get tangled, this might still happen, especially if your dog loves to explore outdoors. To easily remove tangles, you can use a slicker or an oil to untangle debris.

B. Eyes

Another important aspect in grooming your Patterdale Terrier is its eyes. Since the Patterdale Terrier breed has a close affinity to exploring the outdoors, there are times when they end up getting debris in their eyes. If you do not remove the debris, it might cause conjunctivitis on your dog. Simple grooming of the eyes includes flushing the corners of his or her eyes with water and wiping it dry with wet cloth. This is to ensure that there will be no bacterial build up that will form on the corner of your dog's eyes.

C. Ears

Check your dog's ears at least once a week and make sure that the colours inside your dog's ears are pinkish. Also, remove the dirt that adhered to the walls of the ears because this might cause your dog's ears to become malodorous.

A dog's ears are a favorite crevice for bacteria and mites so be sure to inspect them and remove the wax that has formed on your dog's outer ears. To clean your dog's ears, you can use a dog ear solution from your vet or you can use alternatives like hydrogen peroxide, mineral oil and tea tree oil to loosen the wax, as well as disinfecting them. Use a soft cloth or ear buds to clean your dog's ears.

D. Teeth

If you look at many Patterdale Terrier breed information sources, you will realise that this type of dog breed is not prone to getting cavities. Although this may be the case, they are prone to getting plaque buildup that can cause their mouth to smell bad. In fact, it is alarming to take note that 80% of three-year old Patterdale Terriers end up suffering from periodontal disease. Aside from bad breath, bacteria that cause dental problems on dogs can also infect their heart, liver and kidneys

To clean your dog's teeth, use doggy toothpaste and not one used by humans. You may have good intentions of using your toothpaste on your dog but the problem is that the fluoride found on human toothpaste is deadly on dogs and there is no way for a dog to spit it out if they accidentally ingest it.

You can buy meat-flavored toothpaste and apply it gently on your dog's teeth using a cotton swab. Once the toothpaste is slathered on your dog's teeth, you can use a soft brush to gently clean your dog's teeth. Give your dog a treat once in a while to get him or her to cooperate.

E. Nails

It is important that you trim your dog's nails every two weeks. If you don't, then your dog's nails might get splintered and this might cause your dog to have difficulty in walking as it will affect his or her gait or posture. Your dog's nails should not touch the ground, especially when he or she is walking. If you hear clicking when he walks, then it is a sign that you need to clip his nails.

When you clip your dog's nails, start off by stroking the paws to make your dog feel relaxed. Avoid cutting his nails too much because the blood vessels can extend on his nails and if you cut them accidentally, it will cause bleeding and discomfort to your dog.

Make sure that you avoid cutting the bundle of black mass located at the base of the nails. And while you are at it, make sure that you also check in between the paws of your dog. Make sure that there are no cuts and abrasions. Moreover, remove any ticks that have lodged onto your dog's paw if you see them.

F. Bathing

You need to develop a bathing habit on your dog as early as a puppy. However, it is important to take note that you should not give your dog a bath daily. Most dogs, including Patterdale Terrier working dogs, come with a naturally cleansing coat that moisturises its skin and coat, and bathing them everyday removes the body from the natural oil. However, bathing is still important to remove mites and other pests that might be living in your dog's fur. Moreover, bathing is also important to keep your dog refreshed at all times.

When bathing your dog, use a non-slip mat to hold him in place. Also, use a spray hose, leash, a dog shampoo and towels to complete this process. Avoid using standing water to give your dog a bath. You can use a leash to secure your dog. Do not use human shampoo because there might be ingredients that could be toxic to your dog.

Don't spray your dog with water but just wet him or her generously using your hands to massage your dog. Avoid getting water into your dog's eyes, ears and nose. For his ears, you can stuff them with cotton wool to prevent water from entering. Massage doggy shampoo on your dog's fur and create a thick lather. Leave it for a few minutes before rinsing the dog. Dry out his or her fur using a towel.

Feeding Your Dog

It is crucial that you feed your Patterdale Terrier the right type of food and at the right intervals. However, determining the right interval and amount of food can be tricky because the feeding requirements of one dog can vary from another. To make matters worse, the feeding guides indicated on the food bag can be a bit confusing, but this section will tell you all the things that you need to know about feeding your Patterdale Terrier.

Your Complete Owner's Guide

A. How Much Food to Give Your Dog?

The first thing that you need to do is to weigh your dog. Patterdale Terriers can be very difficult to weigh but what you can do is to weigh yourself first on the scales and after taking note of your weight, then weigh yourself with your dog. Subtract the second weight from the first weight to get the precise weight of your dog.

Once you have your dog's weight, you need to look at the feeding instructions on your dog food. Look for the closest weight on the instruction as reference. For example, if your Patterdale Terrier weighs 4 kilos (56 lbs), look for the next highest reference weight in the instruction to get the amount of dog food that you need to feed your pet.

On the other hand, it is also important that you determine the condition of your Patterdale Terrier. Generally, this type of dog breed is very active so they are usually within the range of their ideal weight. However, for dogs that are emaciated, you need to add 20% more on their food portions, while a dog that is obese should have 20% less of their food portions. This is to ensure that your dog is still eating healthily to maintain its ideal weight.

B. Which Plants Your Dog Should Avoid

As a pet owner, it is important that you become responsible for the type of food that your dog eats.

Although you might be feeding your Patterdale Terrier with the right dog food, there will be instances when your dog will be snacking on something dangerous. For these reasons, it is crucial that you know which foods are dangerous for your Patterdale Terrier so that you can screen your dog's food. Foods that are dangerous to your dog's health include the following:

- Alcohol
- Avocado
- Chocolate
- Coffee or caffeinated products
- Fruits with pits or seeds like grapes
- Macadamia nuts
- Onions and garlic
- Xylitol and other artificial sweeteners
- Yeast dough

Aside from these foods, it is also very important that you avoid making your dog eat bones that can splinter his or her stomach and these include chicken or pork chop bones. If your dog has eaten any of these foods and has shown signs of sickness, contact your local vet to have him checked.

Patterdale Terriers might be robust breeds but they are not immune to getting sick because they have eaten something that they are not supposed to. As a dog owner, it is one of your many responsibilities to make sure that your dog is eating safe food.

Training Your Dogs

There are many questions about how to train a Patterdale Terrier. The Patterdale temperament is generally laid back but persistent. Patterdale Terriers are very independent as well as determined, so they are considered to be good hunting dogs and guard dogs. However, it is important to take note that they are not lap dogs, unlike your usual toy dogs. As a pet owner, it is crucial that you know how to understand the Patterdale temperament and Patterdale Terrier behaviour so that you will be able to know how to adjust their behavior and curb those traits that are bad.

A. Patterdale Behaviour

Patterdale Terriers are lovable dogs but they do not like to curl up in their owner's lap all the time. They would rather curl up at the heating duct if the weather is too cold.

Another interesting Patterdale behaviour is that they are excellent diggers. They can dig through gardens or backyards which can cause great annoyance to their owners. Moreover, they are also known to attack any mammal that they encounter for the first time.

Apparently, they are bred to do so as they are hunting dogs. For this reason, they are not to be trusted with non-canine animals because they have the tendency to bite other animals out of curiosity. Although this may be the case, there is still a way for you to train your Patterdale Terrier and cat to get along with each other.

B. Building a Bond with Your Patterdale Terrier

As a pet owner, it is crucial that you know how to establish a good bond with your Patterdale Terrier because it will also help you become successful in training your dog. In fact, most Patterdale Terrier training tips will require you to establish a loving bond with your pet so that your pet will trust you.

Building a bond with your Patterdale Terrier starts the moment you bring your new dog to your home. When Patterdale Terriers feel secure in the knowledge that they are members of the family, they will likely respond to your training commands. There are two things that you need to take note of when training your Patterdale Terrier and these include trust and respect. Trust is all about reliance between you and your pet while respect comes from having boundaries and treating any breach with fairness and firmness. To start a good relationship with your Patterdale Terrier, here are the things that you need to do:

- Spend quality time with each other every day.
- Take your dog out to experience life together.
- Establish mutual respect.
- Develop a way to communicate with your dog using hand gestures, facial expressions or sounds.

By building a bond with your Patterdale Terrier, you will be able to manage your dog better and this will also make your pet calm and well-adjusted.

C. The Four Phases of Training

When training your Patterdale Terrier, it is important that you understand the four training phases that you and your dog needs to undergo in order to become successful. These four training phases are as follows:

- **Teaching phase.** This is the phase where you need to physically demonstrate to your Patterdale Terrier what exactly you want him to do. Dogs including Patterdale Terriers learn by mimicking their pet owners.

- **Practising phase.** Once your pet gets the trick in the training phase, you need to constantly practice so that your dog will remember. Practice makes perfect so you need to be patient with your dog. Patterdale Terriers are intelligent dog breeds but different Patterdale Terriers have different learning curves so you need to be patient.

- **Generalising phase.** In this phase, you need to continue practicing with your Patterdale Terrier but on different locations and environments with less distraction so that he will become consistent in doing his or her tricks.

- **Testing phase.** If your dog has performed with at least 90% accuracy in performing his tricks, you can test his focus by taking him to places where there are a lot of distractions. This will test his focus and resolve.

If you follow these phases, you will be successful with your Patterdale Terrier training but there is also a chance that you will fail. If you think that your dog is not progressing, what you need to do is to re-examine the situation and find out what went wrong during the training. The thing is that training your Patterdale Terrier is a trial and error process so it is important that you know the learning style of your dog. Moreover, it will also help if you have patience during the entire four phases of training.

D. Great Tips to Help You Succeed In Training Your Dog

There are many things that you need to take note of when it comes to training your Patterdale Terrier. Below are the tips that you need to follow so that you will become successful in training your dog.

- Do not scold your Patterdale Terrier if he fails. As a trainer, it is your fault when your dog is not able to do what you want them to do.

- Be patient and persistent throughout your efforts. Never give up on your dog.

- Encourage your dog by giving him rewards like a pat on the head, a scratch on the neck or a small doggy treat.

- Use a cookie, clicker or head halters to get his attention. Patterdale Terriers have a patience equivalent to that of a young child so it is important that you use tools that will get his or her attention.

- You need to make your dog know that you are the alpha so you need to lead the way. For instance, if you are training him to be disciplined while eating, you need to give him food only after you have finished eating.

- Don't let your Patterdale Terrier set the rules. For instance, pay attention to him when you see fit and not whenever he demands.

- Never let your Patterdale Terrier sleep with you on the bed. You need to mark his sleeping area clearly.

- Get your Patterdale Terrier respond to his or her name. You can do this by holding a treat in your hand while calling out his or her name. This partial conditioning will make your dog associate his name being called with a treat.

The point is that you need to establish yourself as the alpha so that training him or her will be easy.

E. Training Your Dog to Socialise

Socialising Patterdale Terriers is a very important aspect in your dog's training. Naturally, Patterdale Terriers are a curious breed of dog and they are not afraid to approach or bark at things that catch their attention. This is the reason why some people mistake them for being aggressive. Below are the things that you can do to train your dog how to socialise with people and other animals.

Socialise your Patterdale Terrier by introducing other people and animals frequently. If your dog shows signs of aggression, you can put him on a leash first and stand by his side as you show him that mingling with other people and dogs is okay.

Walking your dog is also a good way to help them socialise with other dogs. When you take your dog out for walks, your Patterdale Terrier will get used to encountering other people and other animals.

Taking him to travel with you also gives your dog the chance to experience new environments and get used to new sounds and new things. However, if this is the first time that you will be taking your dog on a trip, it might do both of you good if you take a short trip and put him in a kennel and let him observe his surroundings. Never leave your dog's side just to give him or her assurance.

F. Toilet Training Your Dog

Toilet training your Patterdale Terrier is also very challenging because most of them prefer to excrete in random places. The best time to toilet train Patterdale Terriers is when they are young. As a pet owner, you need to be firm when it comes to training your dogs. Below are tips on how you can successfully train your dog to go outside or use his or her litter box.

Learn how to read your dog's body language. Read the signs that will indicate when your pet wants to relieve himself or herself.

Determine their intervals. You need to remember the intervals when your dog needs to go to the toilet. If they are puppies, they might need to relieve themselves frequently and if you own adults, they might only need to relieve at certain times of the day.

Praise your dog. When your dog eliminates in the right place, give him or her reward. This will reinforce your dog's behaviour.

By house training your Patterdale Terrier, you will be able to ensure that your dog will be more disciplined when it is time to go to the toilet. Moreover, it will also relieve you from the stress of seeing his droppings everywhere in your home.

G. How to Train Patterdale Terriers to Stop Chewing Your Things

Chewing is a normal trait among most dogs including Patterdale Terriers. It is their way of releasing their anxieties and stress. To make your dog experience more fun while playing, you need to choose the right kinds of toys. Giving doggy toys to your Patterdale Terriers is also a great way to train your dog not to chew on your furniture or shoes. Below are tips on how to encourage your Patterdale Terriers to stop chewing on your things:

- Give rawhide and hooves. You can give your dog rawhide as chew toys because they are good for their teeth and gums. Moreover, rawhides are also made from natural materials so you do not need to worry about toxic exposure to your dog.

- Do not give old shoes, rock or old children's toys because it will develop bad habits on your dog. The next time your dog sees these things inside your home, he or she will automatically think that it is okay to chew on them.

- Avoid giving your dog either chicken or steak bones to chew because they are choking hazards for your pet.

H. Crate Train Your Patterdale Terrier

Let's face it; we won't always be at home all the time. So we must have one fail-safe place where we can leave our beloved pet Patterdale puppy where he won't hurt himself and our precious belongings. This way, while we are out and about our business, we are at ease that our pet is in a safe place. This is where crate training comes in. When crating your Patterdale puppy, always start as soon as you have your pet brought home. This will also make your pup readily comfortable inside the crate.

Before you start training your puppy, first ensure that you already have the right and proper crate just perfect for your Patterdale puppy or dog. Things to consider for your crate:

- Choose the correct size crate for your pet. The size of the crate should allow your Patterdale Fell Terrier to stretch out, sit or stand.

- Your crate should not be too big that it will allow your Patterdale Terrier to make a bathroom at one end and the sleeping quarter at the other end.

- If you are trying to make ends meet and you just want to buy one crate for the lifetime of your pet Patterdale pup, then buy a crate that is just right for your pet once it reaches adult size. However, while it is still small, block half of the crate so that your Patterdale Terrier won't feel comfortable pooping in it.

- Ensure that the crate is comfortable for your pet. You can place an old towel or blanket to make it soft or warm. Or if your dog is already accustomed to a bed, you can put it inside the crate.

- If your Patterdale Terrier pup soils the old towel or blanket, change or clean it right away to prevent it from happening again. This will inculcate in your pet that the crate is for comfort and sleeping and not their bathroom.

- If you are planning to leave your pet inside the crate for the better part of the day or more than two hours, do not forget to leave a bowl of water. If you are worried about your pup making a mess out of the water, you can buy a small hamster type water bottle and just fill it up with ice.

- Make the crate appealing for your pet dog like placing their favorite toys in it.

Your Complete Owner's Guide

Introducing Your Patterdale to the Crate

Step 1: place the crate in a high traffic area like the living room or kitchen so that your Patterdale puppy will associate the crate with being surrounded by people rather than isolation.

*At night, it is also important for your pet Patterdale's crate to be transferred into your bedroom. The Patterdale pup will be comforted to be around human activity and humans as a whole. Ideally, you do not have to crate your pet until later in the night when it's sleeping time. This sleeping pattern will influence your puppy and will guarantee a full night's sleep for you and for your pet.

Step 2: Never, ever use the crate as a form of punishment no matter how tempting it may get. When referring to the crate, always refer to it in a happy tone.

Use positive reinforcement to cajole your Patterdale puppy into the crate like:

- playing games with your Patterdale pup and dropping pieces of dog food in and around the entrance of the crate. You can also use your Pet Patterdale's toys if he or she is more inclined to toys.

- give your Patterdale pup praises each and every time it enters the crate. Stop whatever you are doing and give him or her full-blown praises. You can give your pet a treat out of your hand, pet him or hug him.

***Avoid pushing your Patterdale Terrier pup into the crate. Let your pet enter the crate during the training stage at his own will. The only time that you can physically and gently manipulate it to go into the crate is during bed time.

Step 3: Feeding inside the Crate can be done once your Patterdale pup is already comfortable entering the crate; as much as possible, place the bowl of food into the back of the crate. However, if your Patterdale Terrier puppy is not comfortable going into the back, start by putting the bowl of food as far back as your dog is willing is to go. Then slowly move the dish further inside each day.

Things to do at this stage:

- while eating and your dog is already comfortable staying all the way into the crate, you can start closing the door of the crate. But, once your Patterdale pup finishes eating, open the door. After doing this a few times, bit by bit increase the length of time the door is closed until you can close the gate for ten minutes.

- Once your dog whines, this only means that you have gone too far too soon; so, close the door for a shorter period on the next occasion. But, remember that you don't let your dog out while it is still whining or else your Patterdale pet will manipulate you next time and knows that whining is the key to be let out.

Step 4: Make your Patterdale Terrier puppy feel at home inside the crate even when alone. The number one thing here is, you must be home when starting this stage of crate training. This will ensure that your Patterdale pup will not relate being in the crate with abandonment and loneliness. Thus, never use the crate when you're out of the house not until when your Patterdale Fell Terrier is fully trained.

Some key factors to consider during this step:

- Build up the length of time that your pet stays inside the crate and try to vary the time of day; it should not be right after a meal.

- Make him listen to your command and use a term for the crate like kennel or bed or whatever you like.

- Once your Patterdale Fell Terrier is inside the crate, close the gate of the crate and sit in the room for 5 minutes, then go to another room where your pet cannot see you for another 5 minutes before returning. Then just sit right in front of the kennel door and wait for another 5 minutes before you let out your pet. Repeat this step several times a day until your pet grows accustomed to the crate for up to 30 minutes.

Step 5: Leaving the Home

Now you are about to jump to a new and higher level of crate training. During the first few months of crate training, you can leave your pet dog when you are away from home for brief periods of time. These are the normal guidelines on how long to leave your pet Patterdale:

- 9 – 10 weeks: 30 – 60 minutes
- 11 – 14 weeks: 1 – 3 hours
- 15 – 16 weeks: 3 – 4 hours
- 17+ weeks: 4 – 6 hours
- You must not crate your Patterdale Terrier for more than 6 hours; the only exception is night time.

Some good points to know at this stage:

- Put your Patterdale Fell Terrier into the crate around 5 to 20 minutes before you leave. Just follow your usual method of crating your pet and maybe leave a treat too. Then quietly leave.

- Do not ever make a big deal about going back into the room or coming back home. Although your pet Patterdale will be happy to see you home, do not reward this behaviour. Instead, after a few minutes of arriving home, calmly release your Patterdale from its crate.

- Once you let your Patterdale out of the crate, immediately take it outside to relieve itself. This action will also reinforce the ideas that your Patterdale pup going to the bathroom will be rewarded.

I. Choosing Collars

There are so many collars and leads in the market it would confuse any buyer. So here is a quick list of the different types of collars, their uses, advantages and disadvantages.

Chain slip collars – these are also known as choke chains and meant for training use only. It is used to train a dog to walk on a leash and to heel. With a quick tug on the leash, corrections are made causing the leash to close a bit on the Patterdale's neck. In general, this kind of collar is not recommended because it can cause damage to your dog's neck. But, if you know and understand how to use it properly, you can use it to train your dog. Do not ever leave your dog unattended when wearing this collar.

Harness – a harness is placed around the Patterdale's abdomen and chest while crossing over the back. At the top of the harness, a leash can be attached. This is best for Patterdale puppies with airway and neck problems. Some trainers believe that a harness encourages pulling.

Head Collars – these looks a lot like muzzles but are intended for training a dog to walk on a leash and to heel. If your Patterdale Terrier pulls on the leash, the halter will make its head turn which is not normal thereby deterring the behaviour. Head halters should not be attached to a very long lead or unattended as Patterdale pups can get out of the collars.

Break away collars – perfect for everyday use with a special safety feature that prevents choking. The collar can break off if the loop gets stuck and your dog pulls away. However, if you hook your leash on both loops, the collar won't break off.

Everyday collars – you can have rolled leather collars for durability and less hair parting or loss for your pup. Buckle collars are preferred for stronger dogs with quick release clasps. These collars come in all colours, styles and materials to fit your style.

Martingale collars – also called a Greyhound collar or slip collar, like its name denotes, it prevents your Patterdale puppy from getting out of its collar while walking. You can tighten the collar with just a tug of the leash but a safety mechanism is in place that prevents the collar from closing completely and choking your pet. This collar is especially suited for sight-hounds.

Metal Prong Collars – these are also known as chain slip collars. Despite its ugly name and harsh appearance, a lot of dog trainers find this collar helpful and effective, especially in training stubborn and strong dogs that have a propensity for tugging the leash. This collar should be used with utmost caution and do not leave your pet unattended when using it.

J. Choosing a Leash

There are lots of leashes available in the market and if you are at a loss on how to choose the perfect one for your Patterdale Terrier dog, here are some guidelines to help you out.

First of all, when picking out a leash you should know for what purpose are you going to use it for, for instance:

- **Training** – for training purposes a cotton webbing of 20–50 feet is the ideal leash. Further, when using this leash, also wear a working glove to avoid blisters and burns from this leash.

- **Outdoors** – a four to six foot length of leash is best to keep your dog in position and paying attention when outdoors. Take into consideration the durability and quality of the leash and its clasp. The leash material—whether corded, leather or nylon—plays a secondary role.

- **Indoors** – a round, thin and long leash made from synthetic material is the ideal indoor leash because it won't get stuck easily under furniture. Further, a lightweight leash will not become a distraction for your Patterdale pup when transitioning from on-leash to off-leash.

Once you know where you are going to use your leash, your next consideration will be the many types of leash currently available. So, here is a comprehensive list of the many types of leash available to help you pick the right one that's most suitable to your needs and for your pet Patterdale Pup.

Standard Leashes

Leather – leather leashes are known for their aesthetic appeal and durability. They are quite expensive and easily chewed by your Patterdale pup. They won't cause any blisters or burns when your pet Patterdale dog suddenly tugs away. A leather leash is more durable than any other type of leash material.

Cotton – a cotton leash is more flexible and lighter than other leash materials. It is best for Patterdale pets who like to pull on the leash. It is also usable in any type of weather like rain, snow or other wet conditions, plus it is easy to wash. The disadvantages of this leash are that it can lose durability and strength in wet conditions, it is easily chewed by your pet and can cause blisters or burns if your dog pulls on the leash suddenly.

Nylon – nylon leashes are the standard material used in leashes and can come in 4 to 8 feet long sizes. It is easy to wash, can be used under any weather conditions, cheap and lightweight. The disadvantage of this leash is that it can be chewed easily by your Patterdale pup and can cause blisters or burns on your hands if your pet suddenly tugs on the leash.

Retractable Leash

Typically, retractable leashes have a nylon cord that can go as long as 26 feet and retract to a shorter length. The plastic handle has a button to help you lock in the length of the leash or retract and loosen the length of the leash as you please.

Neutering Vs. Breeding Dogs

There are many Patterdale Terrier owners who are torn between neutering their dogs or preserving their reproductive capacity for breeding. This section will give you the necessary information that you need in order to determine whether you should opt for neutering or breeding your dog.

A. Neutering Patterdale Terriers

Neutering is the act of removing the animal's reproductive organ so that they can no longer bear offspring in the future. The term neutering is often referred to males while spaying refers to females. This method is the common means to sterilise animals and thus control their population and this will save you— the pet owner—from unwanted litters.

Advantages of neutering

There are many health benefits that you can get should you opt to have your Patterdale Terrier neutered. Aside from birth control, below are the advantages of having your pet go through this procedure.

It reduces sexual dimorphic behaviour in your dogs. An interesting Patterdale Terrier behaviour that you need to take note of is sexual dimorphism such as mounting, urine spraying and aggression. If your dog is neutered, this behaviour becomes more subdued.

Spaying reduces the risk of a mammary tumor on your female dog, thus it increases the survival rate of your Patterdale Terrier. Female Patterdale Terriers who have been spayed have zero risk of pregnancy-related complications like false pregnancy and spotting which can also be detrimental to their health.

Disadvantages of Neutering

On the other hand, there are also some disadvantages if you have your dog neutered or spayed. Below are the drawbacks that you need to be aware of should you let your Patterdale Terrier undergo this procedure.

As with any type of surgical procedure, your dog might suffer from complications like infection and bleeding. Moreover, your dog might also be suffering from a pre-existing factor that may put his or her life on the line. Before you let your vet neuter or spay your Patterdale Terrier, make sure that you are aware of the current medical condition of your dog.

Dogs that have been spayed have a risk of becoming obese. The decrease in the sex hormone is associated to their increase in food intake and reduction in physical prowess.

Some studies have found that neutering dogs can increase the risk of bone cancer. Male dogs are also shown to have cognitive impairment once they reach adulthood because of the low testosterone level in their bodies.

There are many options regarding neutering or spaying your dog and you can always visit your vet to find out which procedures will work well with your Patterdale Terrier.

B. Breeding Your Patterdale Terrier

Breeding Patterdale Terriers is a passion for many people and if you have a purebred Patterdale Terrier that has good traits, then you should by all means breed your dog. However, before you start to breed your dog, it is crucial to take note that breeding them can be time consuming as well as expensive. It is also very important that you assess yourself whether you are ready to breed your own Patterdale Terriers. To breed your dog, here are the things that you will need:

- **Dog breeding area or facility.** If you want to breed your Patterdale Terriers, you need to have a breeding area that will be used when your puppies arrive. Since the Patterdale Terrier breed is not a large dog, you just need a small portion in your house for them to breed and also take care of their young.

- **Know the law.** In some localities, you need to get a license in order to breed your dogs. This is especially true if you are planning to breed three litters each year. Moreover, it is also important that your breeding facility meets the local requirements and that you have applied for the necessary permits to start breeding Patterdale Terriers.

- **Talk with the local kennel clubs in your area.** To gain more knowledge about breeding Patterdale Terriers, it is important that you talk with the local kennel clubs within your area. They can also help you find good resources about breeding this type of dog.

- **Familiarise yourself with the Patterdale temperament.** If you have been caring for a Patterdale Terrier before you decide to breed, it is important that you get yourself ready for the different temperaments that this type of dog displays. This is especially true if you are going to welcome four or five puppies over the following months.

Deciding whether to breed or neuter your Patterdale Terrier really depends on your decision as a pet owner. Hopefully, this section will help you decide how you want your dog to be.

Exercise

First time owners of Patterdale Terriers think that it is okay to just let their dogs run around the garden to get exercise. However, letting the dog play on his own robs you of the opportunity to bond with your dog as well as give your dog other benefits of exercise.

A dog needs to be stimulated in order to be happy, alert and motivated. In order to do this, it is important that you walk him three times a day. In fact,  walking your dog is one of the ultimate exercises that you can do together as dog and pet owner. Patterdale Terriers specifically are outdoor types of dogs and they require a minimum of 1 hour and 30 minutes of walk every day, in different locations. The purpose of walking your dog is that it gets them used to different types of environment and other people as well as other animals.

A. Why Should You Exercise Your Dogs

Exercising your dog is crucial because it helps protect their health. Moreover, this is also to prevent your dog from becoming overweight. Below are the health benefits of exercising your Patterdale Terriers.

- Prevents stress on joints, tendons and ligaments

- Reduces the risk of heart disease

Your Complete Owner's Guide

- Helps prevent canine depression and anxiety

- Protects the respiratory system

- Helps prevent diabetes

Exercising your dog comes with a lot of benefits and it is important that you make sure that your dog gets the right amount of exercise to maintain a healthy body.

B. Types of Exercise to Give Your Patterdale Terrier

So how do you determine if your dog is getting enough exercise? As a rule of thumb, it is crucial to take note that different dogs have different exercise requirements.

However, Patterdale Terriers are exceptional dogs. They may be small breeds of dogs but they are strong and they can withstand harsh conditions, so it is okay to let them do more exercise than other types of dog. Below is a quick guide on Patterdale Terrier breed information related to exercising:

- **1 to 4 month old puppy.** Patterdale Terriers that are between one and four months old can do brisk walking for 20 minutes during the morning. Pet owners should play some fetch with them in the garden for 30 minutes during the afternoon.

Lastly, they can take them out for a brisk walk again during the evening.

- **4 to 12 month old puppy.** When your Patterdale Terrier is between the ages of 4 to 12 months old, you can still do the same exercises for both morning and evening. However, in the afternoon you can take him for a walk in the woods or park for 45 minutes.

- **1 to 2 year old adult.** A young adult Patterdale Terrier requires more exercise than a puppy. You can still take him for a 20-minute brisk walk during the morning and evening but you need to give him varied exercises during the afternoon for about an hour.

- **2 to 10 year old adult.** You can still use the same exercise regimen that you use for your Patterdale Terrier when he is 1 or 2 years old. However, you need to introduce active running to your pet for more variability in the kinds of exercises that your dog does.

- **Senior dogs.** Senior dogs have already passed the prime of their lives so it is not advisable that you introduce strenuous exercises to them. You can still give them a 20 minute brisk walk in the morning and evening but make sure that they get a casual walk for an hour during the afternoon.

Your Complete Owner's Guide

Aside from taking your dog out for a run, it is also important that you enroll him in daycare facilities where he can run around obstacle courses and play with other dogs.

Ideal Environment for Your Patterdale Terrier

Patterdale Terriers are curious dogs and if you leave them all alone in the house, they can create a great deal of mischief. This is the reason why it is important that you set aside a portion of your house that will serve as their space.

However, if you do not have enough space inside your house to dedicate to your dog, you can put him inside a kennel, as long as you provide the ideal environment for your Patterdale Terrier.

Whether you put your dog in a kennel or mark his own space in your home, it is important that you provide your dog with the ideal environment. Since Patterdale Terriers are a very active breed of dog, they are not recommended for cramped apartment living. They are most happy living in homes with large gardens.

They can also do well inside kennels with other Patterdale Terriers but they are not so keen when it comes to living with other types of dogs as well as with other animals. If you own other pets aside from Patterdale Terriers, you need to train your dog how to socialise with other animals.

Taking care of your Patterdale Terrier is very important to ensuring the good health of your dog. However, it requires dedication and immense responsibility, so you need to brace yourself so that your dog will grow into a lovable pet.

Chapter 5: Licensing, Insurance and Microchipping Your Patterdale Terriers

You have just added a new Patterdale Fell Terrier into your family and you have already given it appropriate vaccinations and even bought various things like a dog bed, toys and grooming supplies. Is your responsibility now over? The answer is no.

As a responsible owner, it is crucial that you register as well as insure your Patterdale Terrier. You might think that it is a hassle, why do you need to license your Patterdale Terrier, but the bottom line is that there are many benefits to doing all of these things for your beloved dog.

Registering Your Patterdale Terrier

It is important that you register your terrier as soon as you decide to take one as a pet. This section will discuss what it is that you need to know about registration and licenses of Patterdale Terriers.

Why You Need To Register Your Patterdale Terrier

There are many benefits of having your Patterdale Terrier registered. Below are the some of the reasons why you should do this step as soon as get them from the pet shop or from an adoption centre.

Registering your Patterdale Terrier can help guard against rabies outbreaks. Before dogs are issued a license, it is important that you produce proof of vaccination from a qualified vet.

Getting a licence for your dog can help you save money as you will not be fined if your dog is picked up by a local animal control facility. In the USA, in most states, not licensing pet dogs is equivalent to having a fine of not less than $500 (£300) once the dog is picked up by the local animal control facility.

If you want to travel and you need to leave your dog in a day care or boarding facility, you can do so hassle free, as all of these facilities only accept dogs that are licensed.

The money that you pay for the licensing fees will also be put into good use by funding local animal shelters and rescue centres. Licensing your dog allows you to pay forward the good gesture to other animals. If you love your dog, then getting him or her a licence is a good way to show your love to your pet.

When you register your Patterdale Terrier, you are given a dog tag with your contact information and if they are picked up, you can be reached by the staff from the dog shelter to retrieve your dog. However, if your dog remains unlicensed, your dog may remain unclaimed.

Unfortunately, most shelters only keep dogs for a few days before they are euthanised in a gas chamber.

There are many benefits of licensing your Patterdale Terrier and if you have just bought one, then you should process your pet's registration as soon as you have visited the vet to get his or her vaccinations.

Do You Need A Licence Even If Your Dog Is A House Dog?

There are many people who question the validity of licensing their Patterdale dog breed. If your dog is merely a house dog and does not leave the confines of your home, should getting a licence still be important? The answer is yes. Animals, particularly dogs, are very resourceful. Patterdale dog breeds are very active and smart and they have a way of getting out from a secure yard by jumping over the fence or digging. As a precaution against even worse things that can happen if your dog gets out of your property, you need to register them.

What You Need To Know About Licensing Your Patterdale Dog Breed

All dogs, including Patterdale Terrier puppies, are required to be vaccinated against rabies and licensed once they reach four months old. However, there are times when pet owners adopt an adult dog, so here are the things that you need to know before licensing your dog.

- Obtain a licence for the dog within 30 days of your Patterdale Terrier puppies reaching the age of 4 months.
- Obtain a licence within 30 days of acquiring your pet adult dog.
- Obtain a new licence within 30 days of your Patterdale Terrier entering a new jurisdiction by requesting a new transfer tag.

How to Register Your Patterdale Terrier (USA)

Now you are convinced that you need to get a licence for your dog but you are not sure where to start. You do not need to go to only one specific building to have your dog registered. You can get pet licences at your local animal control facility, city hall or the police department. Moreover, they are also available online.

When licensing your Patterdale Terriers, you need to take note that the licensing fees, as well as requirements, vary from one jurisdiction to another. For this reason, it is important that you contact your local agencies so that you can learn about the licensing process in your area. You can always call the Animal Control Service Department to ask for information about the licensing process.

When you register your dog, you need to do some paperwork to be granted a licence. In general, you need to submit a complete licence application and a rabies certificate. You can also get a lower fee on your licence if you can present proof of sterilisation or neutering of your dog prior to the application. You can also check your local Animal Control Service Department for other requirements so that you can speed up the process of your application.

How Often Do You Need To Licence Your Pet

The duration of your dog licence is only for a year or when the rabies vaccination of your pet expires. In most cases the first rabies vaccination is effective for one year and the licence follows suit, while the succeeding vaccinations will be effective for 3 years.

In most cases pet owners find it very inconvenient to keep track of the validity of their dogs' licences, so most jurisdictions are now selling multi-layer licences so that owners do not need to continuously update their licence. However, if you opt for a multi-year licence, you need to provide proof of all valid rabies vaccination for the length of the licensing period that you have obtained for you Patterdale Terrier.

Licence Fees

As mentioned earlier, licence fees vary from one jurisdiction to another so you have to prepare between $10 and $100 (£6 and £60) to pay for everything. Moreover, the licence fee also varies depending on the condition of your dogs. For instance, altered dogs which refer to dogs that have been spayed or neutered can pay a very low licensing fee because the dogs are no longer fertile. Meanwhile, owners of unaltered Patterdale Fell Terriers need to pay more. On the other hand, many jurisdictions provide discounts on the licensing fees to pet owners who belong to the low-income bracket, the elderly or the disabled.

Paying for the licence fee is very important because the money is used to fund local animal control activities like impounding animals, providing medical attention and running animal shelter facilities.

Getting Pet Insurance for Your Patterdale Terrier

Licensing your Patterdale Terrier is compulsory but is getting them an insurance also required? Getting pet insurance for your Patterdale dog breed is not compulsory but it is nevertheless necessary.

Pet insurance is a great way of protecting your Patterdale Terriers by ensuring that they will get the best care possible whenever they are under the weather. You cannot predict what will happen to your dog and getting the services of a good vet can take a huge toll on your budget. By getting dog insurance, you are not only securing your dog's health but also your peace of mind as well.

What Does Pet Insurance Cover?

There are different types of pet insurance that you can get for your dog but to find the right one, make sure that the insurance policy covers the following things below:

- **Accidents and illnesses**. Dogs are prone to getting certain diseases and also getting involved in different kinds of accidents. Make sure that the pet insurance covers accidents and illnesses of your dogs. The policy should cover the allergies of your dogs as well as hereditary conditions.

- **Routine care**. Taking care of dogs can be very expensive because you need to take them yearly to the vet for a checkup. Moreover, some owners also take their dogs to an animal wellness centre for personal care. Your pet insurance should be able to cover the expenses for routine care.

How to Get Pet Insurance

Getting pet insurance for your Patterdale dog breed is very important but there are some things that you need to consider before you finally sign the contract. Below are the things that you need to know before getting pet insurance for your dog.

Assess your finances. It is important that you determine whether you will be able to afford the policy. Look at the costs that you will incur if your pet gets sick. If you think that you can pay for your vet bills without any problems, then forgo your plan; but, if you think that you will not be able to afford emergency costs for your pet, then get insurance.

Talk to your vet. By talking to your vet, you will know about the medical conditions of your Patterdale dog breed. Knowing the medical conditions that your pet is likely to suffer from will help you better assess the provision for recurring expenses that you will need to make for your pet.

Evaluate the insurance policies. Find out what you can get from the insurance policies that you will be paying for so that you can make the most out of it.

Microchipping Patterdale Terriers

Patterdale Terriers are very active dogs and they have the habit of pursuing many things, as they were bred for hunting. This is the reason why this working type terrier is one of the breeds that usually go astray from their owners. Your Patterdale Terrier straying away from you can be prevented if you microchip your dog.

How Does Microchipping Work?

A microchip is a tiny computer device that is implanted between your dog's shoulder blade and the skin, using a special type of syringe. Dogs that get microchipped do not experience any pain and once the microchip is in place, it can detect the location of the dog through radio waves. In most cases, the owner carries a handheld device that will let him know where his dog is. When the microchip is in place, the dog needs to be registered with the appropriate authorities so that the dog will be easily matched to the owner when found.

What You Need To Know About Dog Microchips

Dog microchips are small but they are very sturdy and they are often made to last forever, so that you only need to pay once to track your dog. When your dog is found by a shelter, the identity of the dog can easily be tracked through a scanner. This will allow authorities to easily contact you once they find your dog. Since the microchip needs to be licensed, you need to pay separate licence fees for the microchip. Lastly, if you change your information such as your address or jurisdiction, you need to update the information on your dog's microchip so that your Patterdale Fell Terrier can easily be tracked if it gets lost.

Ensuring the safety of your Patterdale Terriers is your number one priority the moment you decide to take them on as pets. Aside from looking after their health, it is crucial that you register them as well as get licences and microchips so that you can easily track them if they go astray.

Choosing a Pet ID Tag

Did you know that there is a science behind dog tags and how to pick the perfect one for your Patterdale pet? Of course, aside from personal taste and preference you should take into consideration the following items when picking a dog tag for your Patterdale pup.

The first thing that you must consider is if you have a small Patterdale pup, then choose small ID tags for them. Once they grow bigger, you can then move on to size-appropriate dog tags. The reason behind this is so it will not weigh down your pets. Smaller ID tags still have the necessary four-line information that is important in a dog tag.

The second thing you must consider is: does your Patterdale Terrier puppy have a city licence or rabies tag (USA)? This is important because if your Patterdale dog has two tags that keep rubbing on one another, chances are this will increase the wear and tear of the ID tag. So, for longer wearing tags, choose a slide-on or rivet-on or plastic pet tag.

The third thing you have to consider is that your Patterdale puppy is a hunting dog and of course you want to avoid that jingling noise coming from its dog tag. So the answer to this dilemma is a rivet-on or slide-on tag which not only makes no sound but it won't catch on brush or fences.

After taking all of these items into consideration, you are now free to choose a design and colour that best fits your desires.

Chapter 6: Health Problems, Medical Care and Safety of Patterdale Terriers

Patterdale Terriers are very resilient dog breeds, unlike other terriers. In fact, there are no known genetic problems observed in Patterdale Terrier dogs. This is what makes them very good working dogs because they do not easily get sick. Although this may be the case, this does not mean that Patterdale Terriers do not suffer from any health problems.

In this section, we will discuss the different kinds of Patterdale Terrier health issues that may inflict your dog. Moreover, we will also discuss the medical care procedures that you can carry out to ensure the health of your Patterdale Terrier. As a responsible dog owner, it is crucial that you know the possible medical conditions that your dog will likely suffer so that you will be able to administer the right medical treatment for your dog.

Rabies (USA)

Patterdale Terriers are considered hunters and outdoor dogs, so they have more opportunities to be exposed to other animals, especially other dogs. Rabies is a virus that affects all warm-blooded animals and if your dog gets bitten by a rabid animal, it leads to encephalitis which can eventually kill your dog and also make him or her a carrier of this deadly virus. In the US, there are about 30,000 people who seek medical treatment against rabies obtained from animal bites.

Treatment

For the reason above, it is important that you have your dog regularly take his or her rabies vaccinations. All dogs, regardless of the breed, should be vaccinated against rabies. If your dog has been bitten by another animal that is suspected to have rabies, then below are the things that you need to do as a pet owner:

- If your Patterdale Terrier has already been vaccinated, re-vaccinate your dog and quarantine for 90 days.

- If your dog has not been vaccinated, you need to euthanise your dog and submit tissue samples for rabies testing. However, if you are not willing to euthanise your Patterdale Terrier, what you can do is to strictly quarantine your pet for six months and vaccinate one month before releasing from quarantine.

These are the things that you need to take note of to prevent your Patterdale Terrier dog from getting infected by this deadly virus.

Conjunctivitis

Since Patterdale Terrier dogs prefer to be outside in the sun to frolic, they are prone to developing conjunctivitis. This disease is common among all types of Patterdale Terriers. It is easy to determine whether your dog is suffering from conjunctivitis and below are the things that you need to look out for if you suspect that your dog is suffering from this disease.

- Swollen eyes
- Heavy squinting
- Constant scratching of the eyes
- Heavy pus exuding from the eyes
- Partial or completely closed eyes

Conjunctivitis is caused by a lot of factors but dogs that are always exploring the outdoors get this disease from dirt and debris entering the eyes. Conjunctivitis, although common among Patterdale Terriers, is just a minor disease and it can be treated at home but it is still important that you seek medical attention to prevent the condition of your dog worsening.

Treatment

This particular eye condition can easily be treated by dissolving one spoonful of salt in warm water and pouring the solution onto the eye. Soaking the eye with the warm saline solution can easily rinse the debris away. Aside from making your own saline solution, you can also purchase one from your local pet shop or vet. Applying the saline solution for a few days will help heal the infection but if the symptoms still persist and you think that the condition of your dog's eye is not getting any better, then you should consider seeing a vet to prevent complications.

Skin Wounds

One of the things that you need to know about the behaviour of Patterdale Terriers is that they are feisty and very active. They also love to investigate things, chase small animals and dig holes, so they are prone to getting skin wounds. Skin wounds can be shallow or deep wounds and you can treat skin wounds at home.

Treating Shallow Wounds

Treating shallow skin wounds is very easy. What you need to do is to use cotton pads and a mild antibacterial soap to clean the wound. Rinse the wound with a saline solution to disinfect it. You can also apply an antibacterial ointment to the wound to prevent foreign debris entering it. Cover the wound with a bandage if necessary.

Treating Deep Wounds

Deep wounds are defined as wounds that have penetrated the skin and have cut through the muscle or tissue. For deep wounds, you need to do first aid treatment but afterwards you still need to take your dog to the vet for proper treatment. Before taking your dog to the vet, apply pressure to the wound area to stop the bleeding. When the bleeding has stopped, you should cover the wound area with a bandage and take your dog to the vet immediately. If you self-medicate deep wounds, this might lead to the dog suffering from infection.

Skin wounds on your dog may or may not be lethal but it is still important that you properly address this medical condition otherwise you are inviting infection to set in which can compromise the health of your dog.

Ticks

Patterdale Terriers are not immune to tick infestation and if you do not take care of your dog's hygiene, ticks may multiply within all the crevices of your dog's body. Tick infestation is especially a big problem during spring and autumn.

Ticks are insects that feed on the blood of different warm-blooded animals and aside from drinking blood, they can also be carriers of different types of diseases. Naturally, they exist in the wild and they love to hide in long grass and wait for warm blooded creatures like dogs to run in the grass so that they can attach themselves to the fur of the animals.

The size of ticks found can range from the size of a pinhead to a size of a large bean. The size depends on the species of tick. Tick infestation can cause a lot of inconvenience to dogs and this is the reason why you need to administer treatment.

Treatment

What most pet owners do is that they pull the tick off to detach the head from the dog's skin. However, this is an incorrect way of getting rid of ticks as the head will remain on the skin of your Patterdale Terrier dog and might cause infection. Using a flame or petroleum jelly to remove the tick from your dog is also not advisable because these methods can cause inflammation and irritation on your dog's skin.

The right way to remove a tick from your dog's skin is to place a finger on the tick and gently swirl your finger around the tick in a circular motion until the tick becomes dizzy and easily withdraws from its attachment. At this point, remove the tick and kill it in a tissue or with heat.

You do not need to take your Patterdale Terrier to the vet to have his or her ticks removed. Aside from manually removing the tick, you can also use a tick soap to kill the insect pest infesting your animals. However, if your Patterdale Terrier is exhibiting unusual symptoms of illness due to tick infestation, then you should take him or her to the vet for an assessment.

Fleas

"Aren't fleas and ticks the same?" you might wonder as a newbie dog owner and the answer is "NO". Fleas and ticks are quite different. To give you a better idea of how these two parasites differ, here's a comparison chart.

	Fleas	Ticks
Disease Spread	*Tapeworm *Bartonellosis	*Rocky Mountain spotted fever *Lyme disease *Many other potentially deadly diseases
Climate Tolerance	Prefers warm temperatures	Can endure near-freezing temperatures.
Where they lay eggs	Eggs are shed/laid wherever the Patterdale goes or spends time.	Once the female is engorged after feeding, she falls off, lays eggs and dies on the spot.

How many eggs it lays	20-40 eggs per day for a couple of weeks. Females start laying eggs soon after feeding.	Lays thousands of eggs in a one-time egg laying stint—and dies afterwards.
Who feeds	Only adult fleas feed on Patterdale host.	During a tick's stages of development (larva, nymph, and adult) it feeds on different hosts.
Time on host	Fleas live only on one host and they die on their host.	Most of the life span of ticks is lived off the host and it can survive for long periods just waiting for the right host to come along.
Lifespan	Adults can live for more than 100 days.	One life cycle can be completed in a few weeks or up to 3 years.
Number of hosts	Fewer hosts, which include: foxes, raccoons, coyotes, possums and dogs.	More hosts, which include: humans, dogs, cats, cattle, raccoons, possums, rabbits, squirrels, deer, foxes, lizards, snakes, rodents and birds.

Type of parasite	Fleas are insects. Although it is wingless, it can jump far and wide with its six strong legs.	Ticks are arachnids and are a close relative of spiders. They have eight legs.

From the comparison chart above, ticks are basically more dangerous than fleas. So how do you protect yourself and your pet Patterdale pup from this infestation?

Flea Control

Essentially, there are four basic steps that you need to carry out in order to rid your precious Patterdale Fell Terrier of these irritating fleas:

1) Eradicate fleas within the indoor environment of your Patterdale pup – you can do this by vacuuming your home thoroughly. Give special attention to the places where your Patterdale pup sleeps, under furniture edges and beneath the curtains. Then, seal your vacuum bag in a plastic bag and discard right away.

The next step is to invest in a product that kills adult fleas, eggs and larvae. Foggers are perfect for large open spaces. Surface sprays are for under furniture, cracks, moldings and baseboards as foggers cannot reach these sites. Use these chemicals according to the instructions and take into account the presence of your pets, asthmatic people and children. Consult your vet when picking out the most appropriate product to use.

Clean your Patterdale pup's bedding regularly with an insect growth regulator and an adulticide. And lastly, treat and clean the places where your pet spends time, like the basement, garage, pet carrier and even your car.

2) Eradicate fleas from the outdoor environment of your pup (garage or garden). This generally entails treating your kennel and garden or garage with outdoor sprays. You will probably have to treat these places every one to two weeks. As a precaution, do not spray on places where the runoff could go into fish ponds, rivers or lakes.

3) Remove the fleas from your pet Patterdale puppy. Now that you have begun eliminating fleas from the environment, you can start eradicating the fleas on your pet. There are several products that you can use, such as:

- Flea combs – as you comb the coat of your pet with this product it removes fleas while giving your Patterdale pup good grooming, time and attention. Your Patterdale Terrier will love this.

Your Complete Owner's Guide

- Oral products – tablets are also available that can kill adult fleas on your Patterdale puppy. This is especially useful for your pet if it is exposed to fleas during shows or dog parks.

- Flea and tick collars – a new innovation that is effective in killing both ticks and fleas but has to be applied properly to be effective. In order to get the right fit, you should be able to place two of your fingers between the inside of the collar and your Patterdale Terrier pup's neck. Read the manufacturer's label properly to know when to change the collar, as some products lose efficacy when wet. Some dogs may experience irritation to a certain collar but not to others, so you might have to try out several different makes of products to get the right effect.

- Shampoos – these will help your Patterdale Terrier pup get rid of adult fleas and ticks. For shampoos to be effective, shampoo the pup's entire body and leave on for at least ten minutes before rinsing.

- Dips – dips and rinses should be applied in a well-ventilated area and to the whole body of your Patterdale puppy. While using the product, it is best to put ophthalmic

Your Complete Owner's Guide

ointment on your Patterdale pup's eyes and put cotton ball plugs in the ears. Likewise, you should be cautioned not to get any of the product into your pet's eyes or ears.

- Sprays – flea and tick killers also come in pump bottles or aerosol cans. When choosing a product like this, pick one that has both an insect growth regulator and adulticide. Just follow the manufacturer's instructions on product usage.

- Once a month topical – this is one of the easiest product to use and lasts the longest too. Just apply on a small area of your Patterdale Terrier's back and it works its magic. Some topical products can work on ticks or fleas, or both. So read the manufacturer's label properly to ensure that you're buying the right product.

4) Keep the immature fleas from developing into adults – another word for this step is prevention. And the key to prevention of a flea infestation is to do steps one to three on a regular basis even if your Patterdale Terrier pup is tick or flea free already.

Dental Problems

Unlike humans, dogs (including Patterdale Terriers) do not get cavities but they can still develop tartar, plaque and gingivitis which can all lead to foul breath as well as dental problems. This is the reason why it is so important that you always consider the dental health of your dog by periodic brushing.

Treatment

To get rid of these dental problems, you can give your dog chew toys, raw hide or dentastix to remove the plaque. You can also clean your dog's teeth with a brush.

How often you brush your Patterdale Terrier's teeth depends on your motivation and your pet's attitude towards brushing. This is the reason why it is important to start brushing their teeth while they are still young. On the other hand, below are some things that you need to consider when brushing your dog's teeth:

- Do not use toothpaste on a dog. Fluoride found in toothpaste can be poisonous to dogs. Moreover, they do not have the ability to rinse and spit out so they swallow everything that is put on their teeth. Use doggy toothpaste for your dog.

- When cleaning your dog's teeth, hold on to his head securely and do it gently to prevent your dog from biting your fingers. Make sure that you carefully handle the front teeth as they are more sensitive than the rest of the teeth in your dog's mouth.

- Give your Patterdale Terrier dog a treat every few seconds to reinforce his or her behaviour.

Cleaning your Patterdale Terrier's teeth can be a challenging task but you will eventually be able to work around your dog so that you can help maintain his or her good dental health.

Heartworms

Heartworm disease is still prevalent among dogs. It is a curable disease caused by a filarial worm called Dirofilaria immitis. Although it is easy to prevent heartworms, curing dogs that are infested with it can be somewhat difficult.

Heartworms are obtained if dogs are bitten by an infected mosquito that carries the worm's eggs. It takes about seven months for the dogs to show symptoms of heartworm infestation and for the larvae to become adults. They are called Heartworms because they latch onto the heart, lungs and the blood vessels. If not treated, the dog can harbour more than 250 worms in its body which can grow to a length of up to 12 inches and live for five to seven years.

Treatment

In most cases, dogs show symptoms such as weakening of their immune system, difficulty in breathing and general malaise when the worms have already invaded most of the space in the organs of the body. Unfortunately, treatment of dogs suffering from advanced infestation is impossible and it will only take a few months before the dog will die. However, this disease can be prevented if your Patterdale Terrier is given oral prophylaxis to kill the filarial worms.

To correct the misconception of many people, this disease is not infectious and it needs a carrier – a mosquito – to transmit the disease from one dog to another. This is the reason why treatment of this disease also relies on killing the vector or the carrier of disease. Fortunately, there are some mosquito repellants that you can use to ward off mosquitoes and other insects from getting inside your dog kennel.

Obesity

Obesity should not be a problem among Patterdale Terriers considering they are outdoor working terriers and that they have the intrinsic behavior of playing in nature. However, there are some pet owners who do not allow their dogs to go out and have a few moments to exercise, thus resulting in obesity.

Obesity is not very common among Patterdale Terriers but if you subject this dog to a sedentary lifestyle and overfeed him or her, chances are that your Patterdale Terrier will become obese in the end.

An overweight dog can be a very dangerous thing, particularly to the overall health of the dog. The organs of an obese dog are covered with layers of visceral fats which can be lethal and toxic to the dog.

Treatment

It is therefore important to make sure that you watch the food that your dog eats and that you also allow him or her to run around for an hour or two to get their daily dose of exercise.

Worms

Worms are intestinal parasites that can be any of the following:

Whipworms

Whipworms are caused by ingesting contaminated flesh, water or food with *Trichuris trichiuria*. Trichuriasis infects dogs of any age and manifests itself with diarrhoea, weight loss, anaemia, dehydration or is asymptomatic.

Hookworms

Hookworms or ancylostomiasis are fatal for Patterdale puppies or any puppy breed for that matter. Pups most often acquire this condition from their mother's milk. It can also, however, be caused by larval penetration of skin and is often found in a contaminated environment. The disease presents itself with a pup that has a poor appetite and looks unhealthy, and the linings of the ears, lips and nostrils are pale. Other symptoms include: constipation, diarrhoea, tarry stools, a cough and death is sudden if the pup is not treated right away.

Tapeworms

Tapeworms or *Dipylidium caninum* and other species of tapeworm infect Patterdale dogs through the eating of infected food or through flea bites. Tapeworms can drain your Patterdale pup of nutrition and can sometimes cause anal itching.

Roundworms

Roundworms or ascarids are one of the most common intestinal parasites of dogs as a whole. Your pet Patterdale can be easily infected by ascarids through:

ingestion of infected food like rodents, ingesting of ascarid eggs from the soil, ingestion of infected mother's milk or prenatal infection. In young Patterdale puppies, heavy infestation can cause death or severe illness. Puppies have a pot-bellied appearance, stunted growth, are anaemic, have a dull coat and often fail to thrive.

Treatment

Antihelmintic or deworming drugs are used to cure pets of intestinal parasites like whipworms, hookworms, tapeworms and roundworms. However, no one antihelmintic is effective against all worms. What you need to know is that most deworming products are not effective against tapeworms but are effective against the whips, hooks and rounds. Furthermore, a lot of heartworm meds have additional ingredients that fight against intestinal worms. So it's always best to have your pet checked for specific worms to have targeted medical effects from drugs. But either way this is the recommended parasitic action posted by US Government centres for disease control:

Pregnant Patterdale bitches – they can be dewormed throughout their pregnancy and even during whelping. However, deworming drugs are not effective against encysted roundworms and hookworms in muscle tissue but there are specific medications for this condition.

Adult Patterdale Terrier – deworm every three months.

Adopted Patterdale puppies or dogs – deworm right away with at least two more treatments at two week intervals.

Patterdale puppies – deworm every two weeks from two weeks of age to three months, then deworm monthly until six month of age.

Puppies that have been started on heartworm medicine that has intestinal wormers don't need to be dewormed every two weeks. But remember that no heartworm medicine is effective against tapeworms which your Patterdale pup might get from fleas. So protect your pup with anti-flea medicines or deworm for tapeworms every three months.

Chapter 7: Taking Care of Your Aging Patterdale Terrier

Basically the behaviour and temperament of an old dog is quite the same as when he was a young adult—only that this time age has taken its toll. Your aging Patterdale Terrier may not be as rambunctious as he once was and there will be many other physical and physiological signs of aging.

What to Expect

Of course, just like with people, aging begins at the time of birth but it is definitely not obvious in the first few years of life. In a Patterdale Terrier, the first and most common sign of aging is a decrease in activity level. They tend to sleep more soundly and for longer periods. They also have a waning enthusiasm for games of fetch and for long walks.

Furthermore, they may lose interest in what's going on in their surroundings—even within their own homes.

Skin and Coat

These two also change as a Patterdale Terrier grows older. The pliability of the skin is lost along with diminishing efficiency of the oil producing sebaceous glands. Many other changes occur, like:

- increased intestinal parasite infestation
- occurrence of non-malignant tumors under the skin or inside the mouth
- worsening of allergies
- slow wound healing

Loss of Hearing

A common sign of aging is hearing loss for your Patterdale dog, along with loss of sight. These conditions can easily be compensated by your pet Patterdale even if they are already experiencing total or partial blindness, especially in familiar surroundings. Thus, these conditions may not easily be noticeable to the owner.

Changes in Surroundings and Temperature

Old Patterdale dogs are also affected by changes in temperature and surroundings. If, in their youth, they loved to lie on the patio under the sun or during the winter months, you would now notice that your beloved pet Patterdale is keen on lying on top of the rug instead of on the tiled floor. Sometimes you would also notice that your pet Patterdale Fell Terrier is stiff legged and may have trouble getting up after his nap.

How to Care for Them

There are many ways to ease your Patterdale Fell Terrier's transition into old age. But before we go into that, let me teach you how to prevent your Patterdale dog from aging prematurely.

Preventative Care

We all know that aging is part and parcel of life, but as responsible and loving Patterdale Terrier owners, you can delay its onset through proper management.

Exercise – frequent exercise is of crucial importance in keeping your pet Patterdale in good shape. A fat, couch potato type of Patterdale Terrier may be happily pampered, however your pet may live a few more years longer if you slim it down and take it on a hike. You should know that even old Patterdale dogs love to play with a favorite toy a few minutes a day.

Proper Nutrition – A properly fed Patterdale dog is important whether they are old or young. They should have enough food requirements to supplement their body's daily needs. Thus, a Patterdale owner does try to look for quality dog food and not just that which is cheap or generic.

Other steps that you can take to delay the onset of aging are:

- Check your pet's ears for gunk or odour produced by infected organisms.

- Groom your Patterdale Fell Terrier to keep its coat and skin healthy. This way, you will also easily notice any skin problems like sore spots, body odour, thin coat, brittle coat, or dry skin.

- Clean your pet Patterdale's teeth to prevent gum disease.

Caring for an Old Patterdale Dog

One thing that you have to remember when caring for an old Patterdale dog is not to fawn and over-pamper it. Let your pet set his own limits.

- You can visit your vet for any over the counter medication for your pet Patterdale's stiffness or digestive upsets.

- Do not punish or scold your old Patterdale dog for lapses in housetraining because it's a natural part of aging. You can deal with your dog with a reminder but do not be angry at them because they can't help themselves.

- Install a baby gate to keep your aging Patterdale from navigating the stairs. Your dog is getting older and may already be blind or is struggling with stiffness and cannot navigate the stairs properly. So install a baby gate to keep your dog off the stairs.

- Reduction of calorie intake to prevent your aging dog from getting fat. Previously your Patterdale dog may have needed a lot of food when he was still energetic, but during his or her twilight years, a light diet is more apt. Do eliminate fatty snacks to prevent an upset stomach, you can stick to popcorn, vegetables, fruits or dog biscuits.

- Ensure that your aging Patterdale pet has their own bed or rug so that they have a softer and more comfortable surface to sleep on away from the cold and hard tiled floor.

- If your pet Patterdale is stiff in the morning, do not push him to go outside right away and wheedle him with treats. Just check on him regularly to know when he is ready to go out.

Adopting an Adult Patterdale Dog

There are a lot of misconceptions about adopting an adult Patterdale dog, or any dog breed for that matter. So, first let us bust some myths:

- You cannot teach an old dogs new tricks: this is totally untrue. Dogs of any age can be trained and will adapt to a new home. In fact, rehomed adult Patterdale dogs can become a loyal and loving companion to their second family.

- Another myth is that if you didn't raise a Patterdale Terrier puppy from birth, you're going to be into so much trouble. This notion is far from the truth.

What to Expect

There are definitely advantages in adopting an adult Patterdale dog compared to adopting or buying a Patterdale Terrier puppy. Such as:

- In an adult Patterdale dog, what you see is what you get—in terms of physical and temperamental traits.

- Adult Patterdale Terriers will probably have settled from puppyhood and are not as energetic and rambunctious as they were as puppies. Compared to keeping up with a Patterdale Terrier pup, it is definitely exhausting and you cannot just send your Patterdale pup into his room to play alone—especially when you're having a bad day; this is why getting an adult Patterdale Terrier dog is more advantageous than its younger counterparts.

- A fully-grown Patterdale dog is not likely to destroy your precious belongings and with its longer attention span, training adult Patterdale dogs is easier compared to the frantic and energetic phase of a Patterdale puppy.

Chapter 8: Rescue Organisations

Patterdale Terriers are well-loved working type terriers. The reason for this is that they are very playful and compassionate at the same time. However, not all Patterdale Terriers are lucky and some end up in the hands of abusive pet owners. For this reason, countless rescue organisations were set up in order to help abused or abandoned Patterdale Terriers. Patterdale Terrier rescue organisations are a great way to look for puppies that you want to adopt.

Reasons Why You Should Adopt From a Rescue Centre

There are many reasons why you should adopt from a Patterdale Terrier rescue centre but one of the best reasons is that you can help save lives if you get your pets there. There are about four million dogs that are put down each year and if you get one from a dog rescue centre, you are helping extend the life of the dog that you want to adopt.

Another important reason why you should adopt from dog rescue centre is that 25% of the dogs up for adoption are purebred. This is a great way to look for a new dog, especially if it is your first time owning a Patterdale Terrier. The staff from dog rescue centres are more than willing to inform you about the things that you need to know about the care of your new Patterdale Terrier.

There are many options of Patterdale Terriers that you can get from a rescue centre. For example, if you decide to look for them from a Patterdale Terrier rescue UK centre, you will not only be able to choose puppies but also adult dogs that need new homes. Lastly, adopting a Patterdale Terrier is also cost-effective as they are not for sale. You only need to pay for its registration and insurance.

Preparations before Adopting a Dog from the Animal Rescue Centre

Looking for new Patterdale Terrier puppies for adoption can be a daunting task. If you go to a dog rescue centre, you will be able to choose the right dog from among the many that are up for adoption. To make the task of adopting a new Patterdale Terrier easier, here are some helpful tips that you should do before you take one home.

Keep a pen and a paper to list the dogs that you are interested in adopting. This will also make it easier for you once you need to make the final decision on which Patterdale Terrier to adopt.

Wear comfortable clothes before visiting the adoption centre because if you are going to look for a dog, chances are there will be dogs that will want to get to know you more. Looking for a new Patterdale Terrier can be fun and you also get many extras like a drool on your trousers and some paw prints on your shirt.

Bring other people from your household so that the dog will be more comfortable dealing with his or her new humans. This will also give a chance to other family members to also get to know the newest member of the household.

Dedicate time when you plan to adopt a new dog because a dog is not exactly something that you can easily pack into your car. In fact, it might take a few hours for your new Patterdale Terrier to warm up to you.

Adopting a new Patterdale Terrier from a dog rescue centre has got to be one of the best decisions that you will ever make in your life and it will also make a huge difference to the life of the Patterdale Terrier that you are planning to adopt.

Patterdale Terrier Rescue Centres

Looking for a Patterdale Terrier rescue centre is not a difficult task. In fact, there is a network of Patterdale Terrier adoption centres not only in the US but also in the UK, so finding the right rescue centre will take you a matter of minutes.

When looking for a Patterdale Terrier rescue centre, it is crucial that you look for those that have been in the industry for a long time. Moreover, it is also highly important that you look for a dog centre that has a good reputation so that you can be assured that your future Patterdale Terrier is being handled by good people. Below are examples of dog rescue centres that you can approach should you need to find Patterdale Terrier puppies for adoption.

Patterdale Terrier Club of America

This particular organisation specialises in providing good homes to abandoned and rescued Patterdale

Terriers. They also connect with people and organisations that are willing to find new homes for Patterdale Terriers. (www.ptca.00go.com)

Small Dog Rescue and Adoption

Patterdale Terriers are not really categorised as small dogs but the organisation Small Dog Rescue and Adoption aims to provide rescue efforts to Patterdale Terriers and other small dog breeds that are abandoned and in need of new homes. (www.adopt-a-small-dog.1-800-save-a-pet.com)

Dogs Blog

This is an adoption site for abandoned dogs including Patterdale Terriers and it also has a list of affiliated shelters for dogs. They also provide a matchmaker service so that you can be matched with a Patterdale Terrier that suits your preferences. (www.dogsblog.com)

Patterdale Terrier Rescue

An organisation based in the UK, this Patterdale Terrier rescue UK centre aims to rescue abandoned Patterdale Terriers. Aside from matching Patterdale Terriers with their new pet owners, they also provide medical care to the dogs. (www.patterdaleterrierrescue.co.uk)

Your Complete Owner's Guide

Pets 4 Homes

Pets 4 Homes is another rescue centre in the UK that tries to match pet owners to Patterdale Terriers. Moreover, this organisation also provides products like insurance for your pet as well as grooming kits so that you can take care of your new dog.

Looking for Patterdale Terrier puppies for adoption is more meaningful than buying them from breeder centres as you make a difference to the life of your new Patterdale Terrier by providing your dog with a warm home where he or she is welcome. (www.pets4homes.co.uk)

Chapter 9: Helpful Resources

Owning Patterdale Terriers means that you need to welcome a certain amount of responsibility and knowledge. However, if it is your first time owning this kind of breed, then it is crucial that you know the basic Patterdale Terrier info. Fortunately, the internet is a great place to look for helpful resources about Patterdale Terriers. This chapter will give you great websites where you can connect with other people who are also interested in Patterdale Terriers.

Agility Bits

This website contains information about Patterdale Terriers and links where you can shop for supplies for your dog. Moreover, it also provides links to where you can adopt your very own Patterdale Terriers. (www.agilitybits.co.uk)

American Working Terrier Association

The AWTA is a great place to connect with other Patterdale Terrier owners all over America. This website provides a great avenue where people can exchange ideas on how to take care of their pets as well as breed them. (http://awta.org)

Dogs Blog

Another website that specialises in the adoption of abandoned dogs, you can see a lot of pictures of Patterdales who are in need of a human to take care of them. Moreover, the website also has a canine matchmaker service that connects you to the perfect dog that fits your preferences. (www.dogsblog.com)

Patterdale Terrier

The website contains interesting information and snippets about Patterdale Terriers hunting: including Patterdale Terrier reviews, breeders and famous Patterdale Terriers and their hunter owners in history. (http://patterdaleterrier.info)

Patterdale Terrier Info

This website focuses on the hunting prowess of Patterdale Terriers. It is good for owners who want to take care of Patterdale Terriers and take them to their seasonal hunts. (www.patterdale-terrier.co.uk)

Patterdale Net

This is a one-stop resource that provides useful information on how to take care of Patterdale Terriers, how to breed them and connect with other affiliated breeders all over the US. If you are also looking for Patterdale Terrier kennel clubs, then this site is for you. (www.patterdale.net)

Patterdale Terriers Rescue

This is a great website where you can find out basic Patterdale Terrier information including their habits, origin and care. This website also connects you to different animal homes and shelters where you can look for Patterdale Terriers that you can adopt. (www.patterdaleterrierrescue.co.uk)

PTCA

This is a resource centre about what you need to know about Patterdale Terriers. Moreover, it also gives you helpful links on how to connect with Patterdale Terrier clubs. It is a great place to network with Patterdale owners all over America. It is also a great place to look for a Patterdale Terrier kennel organisation in or near your area. (www.ptca.00go.com)

Small Dog Syndrome

If you need more insight and information on how to address your dog, or perhaps how to avoid imparting small dog syndrome to your pet Patterdale, then this is perhaps one of the most helpful sites on the topic. (www.dogbreedinfo.com)

Terrier Rescue

An online rescue website based in the UK—Terrier Rescue—specialises in working type terriers, including the Patterdale Terrier. The website is also a great place for those who wish to adopt their own Patterdale Terrier and it has a collection of thousands of Patterdale Terrier pictures of dogs that are up for adoption. (www.terrierrescue.co.uk)

United Kennel Club

The UKC is the largest all-breed dog registry in the world and it is a great place to look for Patterdale Terrier kennel clubs in your area. (www.ukcdogs.com)

There are still many other websites where you can look for Patterdale Terrier information and all you need to do is search online. Good luck!

Index

Lightning Source UK Ltd.
Milton Keynes UK
UKOW06f1438010416

271318UK00012B/86/P